Exile or Embrace?

To Bonnie ~

with appreciation
for encircling around
me such a supportive
community — one
dimension of our
wonderful friendship

Mahan
10/05

Exile or Embrace?

*Congregations Discerning Their Response
to Gay and Lesbian Christians*

M AHAN S ILER

The Pilgrim Press
Cleveland

To Janice, Jim, Pat, and Pullen Memorial Baptist Church

The Pilgrim Press
700 Prospect Avenue
Cleveland, Ohio 44115-1100
thepilgrimpress.com

Printed in the United States of America on acid-free paper
09 08 07 06 05   5 4 3 2 1

Library of Congress Cataloging-in-Publication Data

Siler, Mahan
    Exile or embrace? : congregations discerning their response to gay and lesbian Christians
    / Mahan Siler.
        p. cm.
    Includes bibliographical references.
    ISBN 0-8298-1630-5 (alk. paper)
    1. Church work with gays. 2. Homosexuality—Religious aspects—Christianity.
    3. Pullen Memorial Baptist Church (Raleigh, N.C.)—Case studies. 4. Church work
    with gays—North Carolina—Raleigh—Case studies. 5. Homosexuality—Religious
    aspects Southern Baptist Convention—Case studies. I. Title.
BV4437.5.S55 2005
261.8'35766—dc22   2005022480

Contents

Preface

I AM AN UNLIKELY AUTHOR OF A BOOK on the church and homosexuality. I grew up in a homophobic climate, a conditioning I internalized and struggle against to this day. Outside of my immediate family, jokes about "fags" were permitted, along with taunts against Roman Catholics, Jews, and blacks. I lived with the pejorative stereotypes of my Southern culture.

During my childhood I did not know an openly gay person, although I thought I did. The person I assumed to be gay was, in fact, a pedophile. Greg was my counselor at a summer camp in North Carolina when I was a nine-year-old camper. Greg was about forty, with sharp facial features and a muscular body—an agile athlete, a bronze Greek god to all of us living in cabins nearby. The supreme treat was to be invited down to his cabin (No. 25) after "Taps" to sleep by his bunk for the night. At last my time came. The sexual abuse I experienced that night became a secret too embarrassing and bewildering to mention. For many years I interpreted this painful encounter as a homosexual experience.

I held this belief until 1974, when as a pastoral counselor in Winston-Salem, North Carolina, a young man named Stan came to see me as a client. He was a charismatic, gifted musician well-known in the church community. But he spoke of feeling "different" from his earliest memories. In his youth, while other boys were sexually attracted to girls, his sexual fantasies were of men. As an adult, now thirty-four, he knew himself to be gay. I was the first person to receive his self–awareness; he was *the* first gay person to receive me into his life.

Stan, along with a few other homosexual clients, opened my eyes to the particular pain that gay men and lesbians face in our society, a suffering exacerbated by both condemnation and silence from the church. Within the safety of pastoral conversations, I discovered our mutual longing for grace in our lives.

In 1983, I came to Pullen Memorial Baptist Church in Raleigh, North Carolina, as pastor with no plans to address this particular injustice directly. Soon the AIDS epidemic, first surfacing in 1984–85, drew me into the public reactions. At that time, the strongest voice from the church defined AIDS as God's judgment on homosexuals. My experiences with Stan and other gays compelled me, along with a few other clergy, to come forward with an alternative voice.

A circular pattern of growth resulted. The more I spoke openly, the more gays and their families found a safe place in my office and in our congregation. And the more gays and their families invited me into their life struggles, the more I grew in understanding and conviction. Pat, Darrell, Wayne, Susan, Al, Francis, Jim, and others became sources of my conversion.

In the spring of 2001, three years into retirement, I reread the journal entries I had written during Pullen's gradual, at times tumultuous, movement toward its explicit inclusion of gay Christians. These stories belong, I concluded, to the larger church struggling to define the place of gay, lesbian, bisexual, and transgender persons in their theology and practice of ministry. More personally, the memory of these pastoral experiences kept pressing me to chew, swallow, and digest its meaning for my own life.

In the spring of 2003, I sent my journal account of the Pullen story to Pamela Johnson, then editor at The Pilgrim Press. She saw the story as a potential resource to congregational leaders, both clergy and lay, who are raising the question: How will our church be in covenant with homosexual persons? Encouraged by her suggestion to draw upon my work with other congregations who have engaged this same question, I added a guide from which congregations can draw as they enter their own process of discernment.

The nomenclature in this book warrants explanation. GLBT (gay, lesbian, bisexual, transgender) is the currently preferred term. From 1986–92, the years of my pastoral journals, I knew only a few persons who referred to themselves as bisexual. At that time I did not know a person of transgender orientation. In this writing I use interchangeably homosexual persons, gays, lesbians and gay men, homosexuals, and persons of same-gender or same-sex orientation. My writing reflects the nomenclature of those years.

In writing this book I have lived inside of a paradox, for it has been both a solitary venture and a community effort. Never have I been so alone in my work. Yet, this writing carries the imprint of many who willingly read and critiqued my drafts of the manuscript. I expected the solitariness of writing, but I was surprised by the provision I needed and received in full from others.

First, I thank Pullen Memorial Baptist Church and the other congregations who have extended their welcome to include homosexual persons and their families, at some cost, with great promise. I find deep joy in telling their stories in these pages.

My writers' group has balanced critique with advocacy. Bonnie Stone, Lou Rosser, Jem Hopkins, Ann Mann, Ashley Thomas Memory, and Susan Hagberg have been my cheering section along the way.

I thank my two book editors, Pamela Johnson, formerly at The Pilgrim Press, and Ulrike Guthrie who completed the editing. Their consistent encouragement, availability, and suggestions have made my first experience of working with editors an enjoyable one.

The larger circle of critique and support includes Mary Moore, Richard Hester, Pat Long, Peggy Payne, Felicia Roper, A. C. Snow, Rebecca Askew, Nancy Osborne, Jimmy Creech, Bonnie Dixon, Pat Levi, Andrew Lester, Rembert Truluck, Mel White, and Jim and Gisselle Powell. Members of my immediate and extended family have also contributed to this project: Mark Siler, Russell and Jeanine Siler Jones, Colene Siler, and Nancy Siler.

I single out my wife, Janice. She has graciously given time to the book by responding to chapter after chapter. But more than this, she has been a steady soul mate on a journey toward gay inclusion in the church that has transformed our lives.

I dedicate this book to Pullen Memorial Baptist Church, with particular appreciation to Janice Siler, Pat Long, and Jim Powell, indispensable companions on this pilgrimage.

Introduction

HOMOSEXUALITY IS NOT PRIMARILY AN ISSUE. Homosexuality is people who happen to be more sexually oriented toward those of their own gender. Each one in the Preface—like Stan—has a particular name, distinctive fingerprint, unique combination of likes and dislikes. Each one has a family that may or may not accept them for who they are. Like every human being, each one bears the image of God, the grounding of their unconditional worth. To frame homosexuality as an issue discounts the humanity of homosexual persons.

So, how will the church be in relationship with these people, the Stans, Margaretts, Waynes, Susans and their families? This question, being heatedly debated throughout the church, reverberates within our families, among our friends, and in our congregations. I want this book to be a timely resource to those engaging this pressing question.

This book has two audiences in mind. Primarily I am addressing leaders of congregations, both clergy and lay, who are asking three questions: How will our church be in covenant with homosexual persons? Are we ready to talk about this question? And, if so, how might we lead this process of discernment? The marvel of the printed word allows me to come alongside as you explore your responses to these questions. I bring with me the experience of congregations who have walked down this same path.

Also, I'm writing to those of you who are asking a more personal question: As a Christian, how will I respond to homosexual orientation and behavior, whether in my life or in someone else's life? This book is full of stories about persons of faith who have lived this question. Their efforts at finding understanding and defining faithfulness will aid you in your own search.

As I envision you, the reader, I am making some assumptions. First, I assume that gays and their families are present in your congregation, but because of societal and church attitudes, many of them keep secret their sexual identities. I assume that you have questions, hopes, fears, and convictions that you bring to this discussion. I further assume that you believe the church has a unique contribution to make to the current public debate about homosexuality.

If you are leaders, you are responsible for more than your personal convictions. You are charged to provide oversight to congregational life and mission. Because you are leading in a time when this subject is often divisive, you cannot enter this conversation lightly. You must assess your church's readiness. And if ready, you face the challenge of leading a process of discernment that fits the needs and capacities of your congregation. This book will help you do all these things.

I submit that the congregation or parish is the *preferred* place for this conversation. Local communities of faith can address all of the dimensions of this discussion--how, when, where, with whom, as well as what is decided. The discussion is placed within relationships defined by the enduring covenants by which a congregation lives. Questions, convictions, and differences about homosexuality can be offered within the context of shared history and devotion to God that transcends any one issue.

There are other contexts. Typically, high-level committees within denominations are given the task to study this question and present their recommendations. Articles in periodicals, research papers, conferences, and forums further enrich the discussion. However, the results of these content-oriented contributions, while always informative, often polarize more than resolve, alienate more than heal.

How and *when* and *where* this conversation is conducted is as important as what is decided. I propose that a congregation can more easily focus on both the process (the way the conversation occurs) and content (what interpretations and conclusions are drawn). I want these pages to support churches in this bifocal task.

I have divided this book into three sections. **Section I** is a story of a congregation addressing its relationship with homosexual persons drawn from my pastoral journal entries between 1986 and 1992. The narrative describes the incremental movement of Pullen Memorial Baptist Church in Raleigh, North Carolina, toward defining its relationship with gay Christians.

This description of Pullen's experience is not a model to follow. It is not an idealized, cleaned-up account. The complexities, mistakes, ambiguities, costs, as well as the blessings are embedded in the story. I want the journal entries to function like any good story. In these stories you will find yourselves—your questions, your differences, your possibilities, your beliefs.

Every reaction is valuable. Each one will assist you in defining your own faithful response to this contemporary challenge.

In **Section II,** I shift the focus to leadership. I address how to design and lead a process of discernment within a congregation. This effort includes the question of when a congregation is ready for this discussion.

Following my retirement in 1998, I became an observer of twenty congregations that had engaged in this congregational dialogue. I served a consultative role in six of these congregations. Guidelines for leading the process have come from my experience with these congregations.

In moving from Section I to Section II, there is also a shift within me. In the story of Pullen and myself as pastor, I track a movement toward specific convictions about the church's response to homosexual persons. In Sections II and III, my commitment is to you. I want to assist your search for the mind of Christ on this matter. My goal is to strengthen the maturity of your process of discernment.

Section III is a study guide and annotated bibliography for potential leaders of this process. This study guide is designed for an eight-week study group of six to ten members. Themes for each study session draw from the story of Pullen (Section I) and the guidelines for leading a process (Section II). The annotated bibliography highlights written materials particularly useful to congregational leaders.

In contrast to the issues of race and the role of women, the church has only begun the conversation about the place of gay, lesbian, bisexual, and transgender persons in our churches. No question, this dialogue will be on the church's agenda for many years. The rush toward quick judgments that suppress differences will only undermine the reasonableness this complex question requires. I want this book to fortify the patient commitment to discernment that cultivates the courage of conviction, the humility in listening, and the expectation of grace.

According to the gospel of John, Jesus made this promise: "When the Spirit of truth comes, the Spirit will guide you into all the truth . . . and take what is mine and declare it to you" (John 16:12–15). The church does not have a clear word from Jesus regarding homosexuality. He left no commandment about our relationship with the Stans, Margaretts, Waynes, and Susans in our communities. He left a promise and a challenge to discern his Spirit. If the testimonies of these congregations enhance your guidance by the Spirit into the core truth of Jesus, then this book has served its purpose.

SECTION I

The Pullen Story

A Pastoral Journal

THESE ENTRIES IN MY PASTORAL JOURNAL were written from 1986–92, when I was pastor of Pullen Memorial Baptist Church in Raleigh, North Carolina. Each entry was written quickly with little care for wording or style. They were notations intended to capture the impressions of the day. The selections in this book are an expanded draft of this original journal, along with new entries not recorded in my original journal that are my best reconstruction of events, thoughts, and feelings. Most names in these stories and some circumstances have been changed to maintain anonymity without forfeiting my sense of faithfulness to this history.

I also had available to me the work of other Pullen members: Pat Long's account in *Enlarging the Circle: Pullen's Holy Union Process* (1996), and the Pullen Task Force report, "Celebration of Same-Gender Covenants" (1993).

To lift out journal entries that relate to one topic will give an uneven, distorted account of these years of ministry from 1986–92. It can leave the impression that our interest in homosexuality was the preoccupying concern of those years. It was not.

Church ministry is generally unspectacular. It is seldom caught up in controversy. It's about recruiting teachers, repairing the roof, appealing for money, returning e-mails, planning retreats, visiting the sick, burying the dead, and through it all, joining in a common search for meaning with a particular people. Regular life rhythms consume the time and energy of church work: rites of passage from birth to death, Sunday classes at 9:45 and worship at 11:00, weekly choir practice, and keeping the time of church seasons with Christians around the globe. Much about ministry is being faithfully repetitive.

In this selection of journal entries I have teased out some bright red threads from the multicolored fabric of church. Our congregation's coming into covenant with lesbians and gays, like these brilliant threads, was woven into the larger pattern of a faith community active in its ongoing life of worship, learning, care, and service. Yet these threads weave their own narrative in the form of pastoral journal entries in Section I.

CHAPTER 1

The Alarm of Aids

December, 1986–October, 1987

DECEMBER 5, 1986

TONIGHT AIDS BECOMES PERSONAL. At the community vigil this epidemic takes on names and faces. Set aside are the typical safeguards for privacy in a worship service. Left exposed are the open wounds of grief.

Candles are lit for every person either with AIDS or who has died from AIDS. Each one named is known and loved by someone in the congregation. Knowing no one personally, I am the privileged guest of a family huddled together in sorrow.

My assignment is to read the Apostle Paul's favorite metaphor for community, the body of Christ. As I read, the waves of energy from the power of naming seem to wash over us all.

> On the contrary, the members of the body that seem to be weaker are indispensable, and those members of the body we think less honorable, we clothe with greater honor, and our less respectable members are treated with greater respect; whereas our more respectable members do not need this. But God has so arranged the body, giving the greater honor to the inferior member, that there may be no dissension within the body, but the members may have the same care for one another. If one member suffers, all suffer together with it; if one member is honored, all rejoice together with it. (I Corinthians 12:22–26 NRSV)

I'm never prepared for the miracle, how words addressed to a distant congregation in another time and culture can take on life and hope in our time.

MAY 10, 1987

Joan from the AIDS Service Agency asks me to visit Carl. "He wants an understanding minister," she says, "The early afternoon is a good time."

Carl is by himself when I arrive, sitting in a chair, unable to stand and greet me when I enter the room. He has that "death camp" appearance about him. Ribs and shoulder bones are showing through his paper-thin skin. From deep sockets his eyes examine me closely. "Carl expects to die soon," Sue had told me on the phone. His countenance says as much.

His fear erupts through our initial awkwardness. "Am I condemned to hell?" he blurts out. Carl assumes that he is condemned to hell for being gay and for having gay sexual experiences. It's the pulpit message of his youth, and I'm the first minister he has talked to since childhood.

After listening for a while, I suggest an alternative image of God for him to consider. God is eager to welcome us, not condemn. Trust, not fear, is what God desires. "Too abstract," I am telling myself.

Then he speaks about his partner and other friends. He describes the quality and persistence of their care. I see an opening.

"Could your love for Sonny and his love for you, including the care you are receiving from your friends, be a part of a larger Love we call God? God is love. When you experience that kind of faithful caring, I think you are experiencing God."

The connection feels weird to him. Carl is very tired, weary of the fight, and desperately longs to complete his life in peace. The idea of God being with him, to embrace him, not to reject him, seems too good to be true. He smiles at my efforts to console him. Who knows what he tasted in our conversation, or more likely, in my listening.

I leave wondering how much grace had penetrated his layered shame.

MAY 11, 1987

The AIDS epidemic, at first a general concern, became more personal with the vigil in December. Yesterday AIDS became a person, Carl.

The concern has been there for a while. Last spring I felt yanked out of my silence by the repeated Religious Right mantra, "AIDS is God's judgment on homosexuality." In a sermon I identified three destructive themes in that lethal message: combining the fear of AIDS with homosexuality; assuming that all homosexuality is sinful; and the arrogance of knowing with certainty God's judgment. For the first time, I refer to my pastoral counseling experience with homosexual persons. "From their stories [it seems that] some are homosexual as a basic orientation, an orientation seldom chosen or changeable." It was a brief, undeveloped comment.

MAY 12, 1987

Still thinking about Carl. Is there not judgment, as well as grace at work in his life?

During my time with him I spoke of mercy, not judgment. He is full of judgment, full of self-accusing. I am right in pointing to, and, in some measure, embodying a Love eager to override his fear? Yet there is judgment. Carl is experiencing judgment from the choices he has made.

He spoke of times when he engaged in casual and unprotected sex. Only in these last years has he known the joy and security of a committed relationship. There is a kind of judgment being played out in his life, just as there is in mine. Carl and I sit down before the consequences of our choices.

This too comes to mind. Does judgment, whether mine or others' or God's, take into account the absence of safe, wholesome places for homosexuals to meet—say, in churches? Is there not judgment upon the church for not providing caring places in which they can gather? For years, perhaps since its beginning, the church has provided heterosexuals with a welcoming space for introductions and courtship. Is there not a similar need among gays? How hypocritical--the church, refusing to encourage responsible relating among homosexuals while at the same time condemning them for irresponsibility.

MAY 15, 1987

Last week when I visited Carl I was performing last rites and didn't know it. Carl died yesterday.

JUNE 6, 1987

James Nelson's book *Embodiment* is timely. He helps me with the most challenging piece of the homosexuality debate—the Bible. The scripture condemns homosexuality in the seven instances the topic is mentioned. Three of these are questionable references to homosexuality. Only one refers to lesbians. But the hard question remains: How can I affirm homosexual persons and homosexual behavior, even in mature relationships, if the scriptures at no point have a positive word to say about it?

Two points are particularly helpful. One, the concept of sexual orientation, the basic attraction toward either same-gender or opposite gender, is a turn of the twentieth-century understanding. Likely, the biblical writers assume that everyone is heterosexual, concluding that any deviance from that norm must be unnatural, abnormal, and sinful.

Nelson confirms the sense I receive from listening to the stories of gays. Sexual orientation is more discovered than chosen. No one I know has decided to be homosexual. Some say in exasperation, "Would I choose to be this way?" As Nelson suggests, the Bible does not address homosexuality as a sexual orientation.

Second, Nelson notes the absence in the scriptures of any reference to a loving, committed relationship between same-gender persons, unless David and Jonathan's or Naomi and Ruth's friendship qualifies. Interestingly, at one point David prefers Jonathan's love: "I am distressed for you, my brother Jonathan: greatly beloved were you to me. Your love for me was wonderful, passing the love of women" (2 Samuel 1:26 NRSV).

The oft-quoted denouncements of homosexual behavior in Leviticus 18:22, Leviticus 20:13 and Romans 1:26–27 are clear, but there is no hint that this includes covenants between two homosexual persons. Maybe such covenants between same-gender persons were non-existent at the time. The Bible is silent on the possibility of committed, monogamous relationships between gays or lesbians.

Nelson further notes that, as far as we know, Jesus never addresses the issue. This much is clear: the concern over homosexual practice receives minimal attention in the Bible. The abuses of power, the choices of greed over generosity, the neglect of the poor, the worship of false idols—they are the major biblical ethical concerns, not homosexuality.

JUNE 27, 1987

For years I have been moving toward tomorrow's sermon. I addressed homosexuality obliquely when talking about AIDS, but homosexuality by itself deserves a response. It's time for a whole sermon on the topic. I'm giving it the title, "A Christian Understanding of Homosexuality."

In the Pullen newsletter this week I gave a "heads up," announcing in advance the topic of my sermon. I want no one to show up tomorrow and be broadsided. I don't like surprises. I assume others don't either.

A Pullen member, Leonard, calls tonight. He is too anxious to wait: "I just had to express my deep concern for you and for the congregation. I predict nothing but disaster from this!" he blurts out. I am unable to calm him.

Leonard may be gay. He seems to know from experience the hazards of being open about this subject.

JUNE 28, 1987

This morning the sanctuary is full, a larger congregation than normal for the beginning of the summer season. Word has circulated. Few were surprised by the sermon title printed in the worship bulletin.

I could feel the difference when I took my place in the pulpit. The silent moment just before speaking is particularly full. I suspect stomachs are churning. Mine sure is, and for good reason. I am about to speak a truth out loud more comfortably kept a secret in church—that homosexuals and their families are among us, living next door, working down the hall, sitting beside us, active in our extended networks. In all of my years of preaching, I have never experienced such rapt attention.

In the sermon I work with the familiar parable of the Good Samaritan, drawing in part upon Virginia Mollenkott and Letha Scanzoni's book, *Is the Homosexual My Neighbor?* I present the ways in which we victimize the homosexual person in our culture. No surprise in that. Everyone expects me to make the "justice" point.

Then, I attempt an unanticipated twist, the very kind of surprise experienced in the original parable. I remind the congregation that Samaritans were "the most hated, most discredited persons in Jesus' Jewish world. Yet, Jesus presents the despised Samaritan as the hero, the caring one, the source of grace."

Similarly, I reason, homosexual persons, among the "most hated, most discredited persons" in our society, just might be the source of God's grace. Perhaps they are bearers of the healing we need. Only they can help us tend to the wound of homophobia, that fearful prejudice that inflicts blindness and fosters prejudice. The congregation anticipated "homosexuals need our care and advocacy." They likely did not expect the reverse: "we need what only our homosexual friends can bring to us."

As members file out the back door, the responses are noticeably vague. Fine with me. I am relieved to have the sermon behind me.

JULY 7, 1987

The reaction from last week's sermon is encouraging. Andrew took copies for his law partners. The sermon is being sent to family and friends. This was a timely word that some members were wanting. For them, as for me, the AIDS crisis has pushed to the forefront the moral response to homosexuality.

July 11, 1987

Another referral today from the AIDS Service Agency. Eddie is very agitated when I arrive. His mother, dad and partner are present. We meet around the kitchen table, not yet clear of the crumbs from lunch and probably breakfast as well. Dirty dishes are stacked high in the sink. The intensity in their faces sends a clear message: what counts here is Eddie. Eddie alone. His pain, his welfare are all that matters.

"I want you to baptize me—next Sunday afternoon!" Eddie announced with no preparation.

His request, expressed more as demand, comes as total surprise. Avoiding an immediate "yes," I gently probe the reasons behind his query. But Eddie is in no mood for introspection. Neither are his family and partner. They experience my questions as hedging and likely disinterest. Quickly their responses escalate from agitation to anger to rage. Next thing I know, I am hearing: "Get out! We asked for your help, not your questions!"

I'm stunned. I sit in my car for the longest time trying to make sense of what just happened. Where did I go wrong? Did I go wrong? I know that I am the occasion for their rage, not its cause, but still, was I insensitive to their desperation? Should I have said, "I would like to assist in your baptism" and then explore the background to his request?

Regardless, I fear I became another negative experience on Eddie's list of encounters with the church. I don't know that for sure. This is an assumption I make these days: gays understandably carry within them the festering wounds of religious violence against them.

August 6, 1987

Nancy Keppel called me today. She wants me to testify at an open hearing before the Raleigh City Council next week, August 12. The hearing is sponsored by the Human Relations and Human Resources Advisory Committee of which she is a member. They want to document evidence of violence against lesbians and gay men in order to verify the need for legal protection. The committee recommends that "sexual orientation" be added to the city's non-discrimination ordinance.

I decline at first. "What direct violence against homosexuals have I witnessed? None," I tell Nancy. I have not seen anyone beaten, abused verbally, lose children in a custody battle, or fired for being homosexual.

After I hung up the phone, I thought about Eddie, Carl and other gays who have invited me into their lives. Weren't they dealing with violence, albeit more emotional and religious than physical?

I returned the call. "Nancy, count me in."

AUGUST 12, 1987

What a night!

At the public hearing tonight my name is placed at the end of the docket, requiring me to sit through over two hours of testimony. Most of the witnesses are lesbians and gay men who, at considerable risk, report specific acts of violence and discrimination against them. Typical are stories of police abuse, loss of children, unfair job evaluations, lack of employment opportunities, and dismissals for trumped up reasons. Two or three of these stories I could have managed. However, being one of the last ones to speak, I had to sit through story after story after story. The crescendo effect from back-to-back testimonies eventually broke through my well-honed defenses.

Most disturbing are their experiences with the church, especially from preachers. Witnesses speak of pulpit messages that declare homosexuality as sin, an "abomination" before God, worthy of punishment. Even the feelings of homosexual attraction could warrant the wrath of God.

Tonight there was no wiggle room left for sidestepping a conviction that's been forming within me. An alternative message from the church, especially from preachers, must be voiced publicly, and this voice must be as compelling as the messages these witnesses have internalized. It was an ordaining moment.

AUGUST 19, 1987

Today my "Point of View" article appeared in the *Raleigh News and Observer.* It is my first follow-through of last week's resolve.

In the article I describe the public hearing on August 12 as a "coming out of the closet" event for the Raleigh community. I report what was heard—the sequential testimonies of beating, verbal abuse, death threats, and the loss of jobs, homes, and children. I continue in the article:

Some violence leaves scars visible to the heart alone. . . . I found myself pondering [at the hearing] the soft side of violence. It's the violence that occurs from the benign neglect of the many in contrast to the willful aggression of the few. . . . Our silence, our looking the other way, supports the overt violence against the homosexual in our community. Our refusal to speak leaves a vacuum in which the voices of condemnation and prejudice reverberate unchecked.

SEPTEMBER 14, 1987

Nancy wants more. She calls this afternoon, insisting that I come to a meeting of clergy tomorrow. She, along with a few of us, hung around after the hearing on August 12 expressing the clear need for an alternative clergy voice. She's doing what she does best, herding church leaders, especially pastors, toward social action.

SEPTEMBER 25, 1987

This group has promise. I looked around the Fairmont Methodist conference table today and saw clergy representing most of the denominations—Jim, Episcopalian; Jimmy, Methodist; Steve, Lutheran; Charlie, Roman Catholic; Alan, Presbyterian; Morris, Unitarian Universalist; Cally, David, and Nancy, United Church of Christ; and me, Southern/American Baptist. And there is energy around this circle. Most of us were present at the public hearing and feel similar reactions—outrage over a silent church.

The defining question became: How can we, as representatives of faith communities, raise the level of consciousness about the pervasive, destructive affects of homophobia? We finally settle on a name—Raleigh Religious Network for Gay and Lesbian Equality (RRNGLE).

CHAPTER 2

The Power of Story
November, 1987–June, 1988

November 10, 1987

I HAVE ENTERED AN UNDERGROUND WORLD. What's been invisible is coming to light. Take Paul, for example. In knowing him for five years, I never realized until yesterday what he faces from day to day. He's a schoolteacher in a rural setting. If discovered, Paul would likely be ousted at a moment's notice. So he works creatively to protect his secret. To avoid the suspicion of his orientation he takes a woman friend to the school dances. With the other male teachers he makes sure to laugh at their "fag" jokes. He is on guard constantly. All this to secure the privilege of teaching.

Heterosexism may be deeper, or at least more complex, than racial prejudice. If we are African American, Hispanic or Caucasian, we know our race. We know to what group we belong. Kinship is visible. That's not true for Paul.

January 4, 1988

Another face to homosexuality appeared today. Jim and Francis from High Point came to see me upon recommendation of a mutual friend. They seem unaccustomed to asking for help. His tasteful plaid sport coat, her beige wool suit and, in general, their presenting presence communicates privilege. They could be my parents in an earlier day. They could be Janice and me. Today desperation drove them the eighty-five miles from High Point to Raleigh.

Jim's opening words: "Pastor, our daughter, Beth, told us last Saturday that she is lesbian." He lets that news sink in for a few moments, and then continues: "We had no clue that she is homosexual. We don't know any gays. Of course, we have seen pictures of their gaudy dress and 'in your face' deviance, but our daughter is not that way!"

Francis adds: "And we don't know what to do. Where can we go? We certainly cannot tell our friends. And our pastor? Well, we like him, but we don't feel comfortable talking with him—about this. So we called Roy. He said you would talk to us."

Jim and Francis are in the first stages of responding to a devastating loss, all the more traumatic because this loss is unexpected, unacceptable and unspeakable. In their mind, at this point, they have lost a daughter. Suddenly, all of their dreams for Beth have turned to nightmares—no "normal" career, no marriage and children, no grandchildren. Gone is their imagined future, both hers and theirs.

It's the image of Beth that is shattered, not Beth, but that's not a distinction they can see today. Jim and Francis are asking for someone to be with them in their grief, sit with them in their shock, disappointment and guilt. Yes, the guilt kicked in: "What did we do or not do to cause this?"

They agree to come back next week.

January 5, 1988

A good day. The Raleigh City Council added "sexual orientation" to its anti-discrimination ordinance protecting city employees and the employees of contractors with the city. Perhaps the public hearing last September made a difference.

January 11, 1988

Francis and Jim return today. The shock of Beth's announcement is easing. We share our histories on the topic of homosexuality, what we heard and internalized as children, what our experiences have been as adults. Their upbringing is as homophobic as mine, but absent for them is someone to offer the gay perspective. Now they have Beth.

Francis and Jim are exceptional. From what I hear, many parents of gays are not willing to face their own feelings and attitudes. They either abandon their children or choose to deny reality, reverting to a "don't ask, don't tell" policy. I mention to Francis and Jim the resource of PFLAG (Parents and Friends of Lesbians and Gays). They flinch, not ready for that step. I remain the only one, except for our mutual friend Roy, who knows their struggle.

FEBRUARY 2, 1988

My theology is changing—not so much my understanding of God as my understanding of evil.

My life of privilege has protected me from the raw, sharp edge of oppressive power. Borrowing an image from another minister, I was born and reared on the Pharoah side of the liberation movements of our time. My growing awareness of heterosexism, however, is thrusting me into the power of oppression. With Dan today I feel up against a destructive force that has him in its grip. "Evil" is the only word strong enough to name it.

Dan is the casualty of a stern, moralistic religious childhood. His self-despising is an open wound that won't heal. From a deep place he announces to me: "I am an 'abomination' to the Lord. I know I am, although I've not been involved with anyone. Not that I don't want to, but I am too scared. My fantasies torment me."

It's seldom this clear, but with Dan I felt myself up against a formidable power. I was in a face off with those self-accusing demons that roam his inner landscape. I was, in Paul's words, "struggling, not against flesh and blood, but against . . . the cosmic forces of this present darkness, against the spiritual forces" [Ephesians 6:12 RSV].

And inside Paul's metaphor, I pictured myself putting on "the whole armor of God." That is, I claimed all of the pastoral authority he was expecting of me. I assumed a power I didn't feel. He saw me as a "man of God," and I accepted every ounce of his projection. With all of the audacity in my role, I spoke a counter word to the lie at root within his soul. "Dan, you are not an abomination. You are not condemned for being the way you are. What you are telling yourself is a lie. Whether you feel it or not, you are a child of God, embraced by God, made in God's image and therefore capable of loving, creating, and contributing."

Afterward we sat together for a few minutes, both of us feeling the aftershocks of such a possibility. I try to imagine his inner dialogue: Is this possible? Could the pastor be right? What if I believed this? How can he be so sure?

He stays with the silence for a while, expresses thanks for the time, saying as he leaves that he has a lot to consider. He promises to be in touch.

Tonight I am trying to make theological sense of what happened. In those moments with Dan I was doing battle against years of social and religious conditioning. A huge intricate web of re-enforcing beliefs hold Dan in bondage. These enslaving voices exceed the opinions of a "flesh and blood" person or two. They represent a mindset, a way of seeing assumed by many. These repeated messages have garnered sufficient force to undermine his sense of worth. I was competing against a determined resistance to any blessing in God's name.

FEBRUARY 15, 1988

Francis and Jim from High Point continue to come. They are still unable to share their pain with friends or family.

Clearly, Beth is their best resource. Beth, a graduate student in a nearby university, is mature beyond her years. She seems gentle and caring with her parents. It took years for Beth to understand her sexuality. Her parents are taking a crash course.

FEBRUARY 21, 1988

Darrell comes into my life today and exits just as quickly. I will not forget him.

He called last week for an appointment. When I asked him over the phone what he wanted, he dodged a clear answer, only repeating, "I need to see you."

Darrell is visibly nervous as he enters my office this morning. He avoids eye contact as he shakes my hand perfunctorily. His dark, pin-striped suit, starched white shirt, paisley tie and polished black shoes announce a person accustomed to executive quarters.

Once in his chair, he draws the parameters of our conversation. "I want only this hour with you. I don't expect to see you again. I am here because I want one other person to know the truth about me. I am homosexual."

He takes a deep breath, relaxing slightly. He had said the hardest part. He continues, "I cannot carry this secret any longer. I thought, maybe if another human being knew this about me, I wouldn't feel so lonely." I am struck by his reference to me as "another human being." He is not asking for a relationship.

Darrell leans back into the chair, slows the pace of his talking and tells me about his growing up years in rural South Carolina. Influences on him as a child included a Primitive Baptist congregation. In his early adolescence, he began to look for ways to break free from the constrictions of his background. College provided the way. There he was able to acknowledge to himself, but to no one else, his strong sexual attraction to his roommate. Upon graduation, he turned to marriage with the hope that marital intimacy would erase the homosexual fantasies. It hasn't.

Now he is CEO in a regional clothing business, still married, with two adolescent daughters and serves on the vestry in his church. "I would lose everything if people knew. Nobody in my family, and probably in my business and church, would understand."

He continues for a while before I ask, "Does your wife know?" "Yes, she knows. I don't want her to believe that our lack of sex is her fault."

We explore for a few minutes the role of his faith. He doesn't express the kind of religious self-loathing that I often have heard from other gay men. "I feel at peace with God. He understands. My loneliness comes with people, not with God."

When the hour has passed, Darrell stands up, says, "Thank you," and leaves abruptly, reminding me at the door that he never plans to see me again.

Darrell left my office this morning; he did not leave my mind. I try to imagine what it would be like being Darrell—the profound loneliness, the fear of being discovered, the sense of being two persons, the repression and likely depression, and the secret pact with his wife. A solitary confinement.

MARCH 12, 1988

Our first RRNGLE conference today . . . and at Pullen. We hosted the first religious conference ever held in North Carolina for the purpose of bridging the gap between gay/lesbian persons and mainline churches/synagogues. The participants, a hundred plus, are well divided between straight and gay.

Max is in the conference. I knew him as a child in Winston-Salem. "This is the first time I have been in church for eighteen years," he tells me. "I can't believe I am here in a Baptist church!" He is one of many gays who risk coming to an all-day meeting sponsored by a religious organization and held in a church.

We are all feeling some risk. This is a RRNGLE "coming out" event as well. I could feel the ebb and flow of fear and excitement throughout the day. I think of Rudolph Otto's classic, *The Idea of the Holy*. His description of the holy experience as *mysterious tremendum et fascinans* describes today's conference. According to Otto, a sacred event is mysterious, defying words; it makes you tremble with awe and unknown implications; and it is fascinating, drawing you into its transforming power. In this sense today's conference is holy. We encountered Mystery; we trembled; and we felt drawn into invigorating energy.

Cally facilitates the "fish bowl," a high point of the day. Eight chairs are placed in a circle. Then she invites eight persons to volunteer, sit in the circle and tell their personal stories about homosexuality. The ground rule: no debate is permissible. When a story is shared, the others in the circle and audience are to listen with respect, receiving the personal experience as a gift. Then after persons speak, they return to the audience, freeing a place for another to join the circle.

Heterosexuals in the circle speak of their struggle with homophobia. Homosexual participants share their bouts with self-hatred and their breakthroughs into self-acceptance. A few parents break their silence, describing the experiences with their children who are gay or lesbian. Still others enter the circle to name their questions and ambivalence.

Today a truth comes into focus: Personal stories have the power to undermine stereotypical thinking. They take us beneath the usual polarities that prohibit dialogue, polarities like oppressor/victim, righteous/sinner, good/bad, saved/condemned, and even gay/straight. By listening reverently to each other, regardless of the content, stories take us to our life together. The vulnerability in story telling, more than persuasion and debate, carries the hope of transformation.

April 11, 1988

At the beginning of our scheduled visit, Susan introduces herself to me as a lesbian, a daughter of a Southern Baptist pastor in Missouri. Her question to me: "Should I remain celibate?" She had talked with her pastor (not her father). He accepted her orientation as a given but insisted that she be celibate. She wants to know what I think.

She tells me about her life, including her relationship with her father and her current pastor, plus the way she is trying to make sense of being both lesbian and Christian. Convinced by her genuineness, I offer my perspective.

"I think celibacy is a calling. Many Christians through the years have seen celibacy as a way to enhance their singular devotion to Christ. Celibacy can be chosen as a discipline of discipleship. However, from what you tell me, your pastor wants to make this choice for you. I hope you will continue to discuss this with those whom you respect and then make your own decision."

Her pastor represents the point of view that's widespread: If you are homosexual, you must not express homosexual sexual behavior. I left Susan with what I consider the more important question: Whatever our sexual orientation, how do we take responsibility for our gift of sexuality? Celibacy is one option.

MAY 11, 1988

The pastoral visits with gay men, mostly non-Pullen members, have picked up again for some reason.

They usually want my thinking as a pastor about homosexuality. Then they compare my content with what they hear from other ministers. It's a life project for them. They are researching the question: Can I reconcile my sexual identity with my Christian faith?

Like Al today, most of these men are from religious backgrounds that take the Bible literally. I'm a puzzle to them. When it is so clear that Leviticus declares homosexual behavior as "abomination" to God, even punishable by death, how could I, as a pastor, not conclude that homosexuality is a sin? That is Al's question.

For most Christians, the first issue in a conversation about homosexuality is the question of hermeneutics. How do we interpret the Bible?

I said something like this to Al. "There are two basic ways of understanding the Bible. Both take God seriously. Both grant primary authority to scripture. Both look to Jesus as the clearest revelation of God's nature. And both listen for the Word of God that addresses us in the reading of scripture.

"One way regards the Bible as a divine creation, written by God. This way sees the Bible as factual truth, each word the Word of God.

"The second way sees the Bible as inspired human responses of two religious communities, Israel and the early church, to God's blessing and call to shalom. This approach to scripture includes the historical understanding of passages and appreciates the importance of myth, story, and metaphor as conveyers of truth." I wasn't that crisp and concise with Al, but that's the gist of my mini-lecture.

By first focusing on our assumptions about biblical interpretation, we both are more willing to consider respectfully each other's point of view. He surprises me with his curiosity. I surprise him with my love for the scriptures. When we came to the discussion of homosexuality, the threat of the conversation seemed reduced a bit.

Al's intellectual work, while important, is limiting. I wish I knew a mature gay member in our congregation to whom I could refer Al, someone who could offer friendship and guidance. He needs a mentor.

May 23, 1988

Today is another first. Jan is the first lesbian member of Pullen to tell me her story.

"I want you to be aware of my family situation," Jan establishes at the outset of our visit this afternoon. "I'm not coming with a problem to be solved." Jan has discovered that her strongest sexual attraction is toward women, not men. She assumes that she is lesbian, or at least bisexual. She is married to Sam and they have a precocious, six-year-old Michael. All three are moderately active in our congregational life.

"I admire my husband. We have a friendship that I value, but I have no desire to have sex with him," she continues. "I haven't for years."
Then she tells me of attending a woman's conference where she experienced strong sexual attraction toward a few other women. She came away with disturbing questions about her sexuality. She suspects that she is lesbian.

I ask her if Sam is aware of her inner struggle. "Yes, he is. We are open with each other about most things." At this point they both want to continue in the marriage. As she put it: "I intend to be faithful to him and to our mutual parenting of Michael."

She asks if she could talk with me from time to time. "It helps to talk with someone who knows." I feel hesitant. "We'll see," I remember telling her. "I want to be your pastor, but I strongly urge you and Sam to consider seeing a pastoral counselor. This would provide a safe place, with skilled care, for regular communication to continue." She promises to consider the option.

When she's gone, I'm left with the sense of wading deeper and deeper into these waters. The more involved I become, the more complex "church facing homosexuality" becomes. Jan is a married woman with strong same-sex attractions. There must be many others like Jan.

JUNE 25, 1988

There is something powerful about putting your body where your mouth is. I took that step today, literally, by walking in my first Gay Pride March, hoisting our RRNGLE banner along with Jimmy and Jim.

The march carried me well beyond my comfort zone. I felt exposed. Where is the black robe to cover me? Where is a pulpit to stand behind? Walking in the open before the TV cameras and jeering crowds feels vulnerable in the extreme.

"Pride" is a fitting name for the march. I am proud to be with both gay and straight in common cause. And it's liberating to be free of ambiguity with clear lines drawn between right and wrong. As I walk today, the lines are literally clear. We are marching in a straight line toward the capitol building, and the crowd, mostly hostile, is lined up along the way shouting, "Faggot lovers," lifting high their placards, "Abomination to God." Indeed, the lines are clearly drawn.

I am thinking as I walk, this is a dangerous clarity—right against wrong, good against evil, righteousness against sin. Interestingly, those on both sides of this line believe themselves to be right, good, faithful, and righteous. Everyone is claiming the high moral ground.

"Pride" then has a double edge for me. Yes, I feel pride in associating with these courageous souls who risk declaring who they are and what they believe, not just in an annual march, but day in and day out. But pride is seductive. It converts so subtly in me to self-righteousness. As I walk, can I see these angry bystanders as human beings? Can I imagine the enormous pain and fear that must lurk beneath the abhorrence in their speech? Is not their outrage rising from their sense of God's will? The force of their conviction is so strong that they, as we, are willing to devote the heart of a Saturday to its expression.

JUNE 26, 1988

I took a risk in today's sermon. This was the third sermon in a series on human sexuality. The first two were on the topics of marriage and divorce.

Someone in the congregation accurately predicted that in this morning's message I would address in some way the church's response to homosexuality. This person wrote me a letter that I received last Wednesday. This is the risk. I decided to include the letter in my sermon.

> Dear Mahan,
>
> Some of us, whom the church has driven to pretense or exile, are waiting to hear whether we are really the children of God or merely the skeletons in the family closet. Are we, too, made in the divine image, or are we some grotesque cosmic error? The crucial issue is not what we do or refrain from doing. That is a different matter. The issue is what we are, and whether our acceptance as participants in the community of faith is, as it often seems, contingent upon our not letting others know who we are. We have no record of Jesus' having spoken directly to our situation. The Old Testament and the Southern Baptist Convention are unequivocal. Is "abomination" the final word? I await your sermon next Sunday in hope and terror.
>
> With deep respect,
> A Familiar Stranger

I read the letter as part of the sermon and then responded:

> Sexual orientation is innate, a given, part of our being. How cruel of the church to judge as "abomination" what God has given in the creation of a person. How cruel of God to allow some to be inherently homosexual, yet condemn any acknowledgement and responsible, caring expression of that gift.

Tonight I am wondering: Have I violated this person's trust by reading the letter? As people kept filing by me at the conclusion of the worship service this morning, I hoped that the writer of the letter would identify himself. Or, is this person a woman? I looked for some indication of the author, but detected none.

JUNE 27, 1988

I still don't know who the letter's author is. Have I destroyed that person's confidence in me by being open with what was given to me privately? Even though the letter is anonymous, I shared it publicly without permission. Yet the letter was so well written, so on target with the issue of condemnation or acceptance. I couldn't resist reading it.

JUNE 30, 1988

What a relief! Pat Long breaks the silence. She comes by the office this afternoon to identify herself as the "Familiar Stranger."

She reports feeling more surprise than anger over my including her letter in the sermon. "Shock" is her word. She hasn't been sure what my position on homosexuality might be. My previous sermon on the topic in '86 was during a time of her absence from Pullen. She describes sitting in the choir with no inkling that I would incorporate her question in my message. Even though no one knew of her authorship, she felt exposed.

When I begin to apologize, she stops me. She wants me to know that the sermon signaled a turning in her life. Pat has never heard from a minister what she knows to be true: sexual orientation is innate, a given, a part of our being. The message, she says, got through to her core. She is loved by God as she is. She heard it, really heard it for the first time.

CHAPTER 3

Public Reactions

July, 1988–July, 1989

JULY 19, 1988.

FOR A MONTH I HAVE BEEN STEWING about the resolution on homosexuality passed by my denomination during our national convention in June. The Southern Baptist statement condemns homosexuality as "deviant," "a manifestation of depraved nature," and "a violation and perversion of divine standards." This is my faith family talking!

Our state Baptist paper rejected my written response, but Jack Harwell, editor of *Southern Baptists Today,* is interested. He is willing to publish my point of view.

AUGUST 10, 1988

In the *Independent Weekly,* B. Jay Gladwell responded to our RRNGLE paid advertisement for lesbian and gay equality. He saw this as "another indicator of the growing moral degradation of the religious community as well as society in general." He sees those of us who signed the ad as doing "a great injustice" to ourselves, society, and the religious organizations that we represent.

On behalf of RRNGLE, I answered Mr. Gladwell. In a letter to the editor I included my convictions about the Bible and homosexuality that had formed over these last years. Then I ended with an appeal to move beyond a proof-text approach to scripture.

> Clearly, homosexuality is not a prominent concern in the Bible. I suspect that our culturally induced fear and repulsion of homosexuality prompts us to generalize upon a few selected passages. Surely the greater biblical mandate is to understand homosexual persons—to confront behavior when it is destructive, to feel the pain of their oppression, to confess our guilt as reli-

gious communities in our participation of their victimization, to support ways by which their gift of sexuality can be expressed in constructive, life-giving ways, and to learn and be enriched by their storied struggle for freedom and equality.

SEPTEMBER 13, 1988

Today my article in *SBC Today* arrived. The article is an appeal for a pastoral response to homosexual persons. I call for a time of listening and dialogue, not a time for the kind of pronouncements passed by the Southern Baptist Convention in June.

In the article I include Pat's letter signed as "A Familiar Stranger," the one I read in the sermon last June. With her letter as a backdrop, I raise these questions:

Imagine, with the "familiar stranger," hearing over and over that homosexuality is a sin, knowing that you did not choose to be a homosexual. Or, what would it be like growing up feeling peculiar, different, a misfit, finding it so hard to love yourself, to feel loved by others or even by God? How would it be to visit your family, feeling the continued pressure to conceal that dimension of who you are?

Imagine the dilemma of struggling constantly with the decision to tell or not tell . . . whom can I trust . . . what is the cost of opening the "closet door"? . . . if I come out of the closet, will I have to come out of the church as well? . . . How would it be to hold a public office, or a controversial job always wondering if your homosexuality would be discovered and used against you?

Can we grasp the experience of being seen through reflected rays of the typical stereotypes? The stereotypes are all too familiar: all gay men are effeminate; lesbians are haters of men; all homosexuals are neurotic, immature and irresponsible; they know nothing of love, only lust; homosexuals are responsible for AIDS; they are out to molest children and undermine the family.

I end the article with an appeal:

Let our Christian responses to homosexuality be shared clearly, boldly, gracefully, humbly in the best spirit of our Baptist heritage of free expression. Homosexuality is not an "issue"; it is people. As a pastor, drawing from pastoral experience, I urge that we listen to the voice of God—not only in one another's witness, not only in the witness of scripture, but also in the storied struggle of our neighbor, the gay man and lesbian in our midst.

OCTOBER 20, 1988

What a surprise this morning to read in the *Raleigh News and Observer* the announcement of our termination as adjunct faculty at Southeastern Baptist Theological Seminary. Janice and I assumed that the renewal of our contract would be automatic. There was no hint of this coming. Without notice our years of teaching a marriage enrichment class are over.

I laid the newspaper down and began to count on my fingers the classes I have taught or co-led over the years. I came up with twelve seminary courses, beginning, I think, in 1977. And now, a newspaper article carries the word of our dismissal. Not a call. Not a letter.

The reason? Of course, it's my stance on homosexuality. The article quotes President Drummond saying I "affirm gay lifestyle." There's irony here. Our courses on marriage enrichment never address the subject of homosexuality. It's my writing, not my teaching that disqualifies—*us*. The article in *SBC Today* must have given my opponents on the board of trustees the ammunition they need. Janice is guilty by association.

I will call President Drummond and ask for an appointment. Janice prefers that he come to our home.

OCTOBER 30, 1988

President Drummond, along with Dean Worley, came for lunch today. Even before the meal was served, he apologized for not communicating with us directly about our dismissal. "I regret that you heard about the trustees' decision from the local paper."

"That's insensitive but minor," I respond. "Major for me is the accusation—'Siler affirms gay lifestyle.' This is code language for promiscuous sex among homosexuals, the very opposite of my position. I support responsible sexual behavior among both homosexual and heterosexual persons within committed relationships. But the damage is done. Your lie has gone out through the media."

He didn't seem to understand my grievance. "So it's true that you would affirm, even bless a relationship between two homosexuals?"

"I haven't but I probably would if they thoughtfully entered into covenant with each other before God and the church. It's something I am thinking about."

"Well then, we cannot have anyone teaching at Southeastern who does not believe in the clear biblical mandate that homosexual sexual behavior is sinful in any context."

"Certainly," I acknowledge, "the seminary must have theological standards for teaching. I understand that I fall outside of these parameters. But this is not my complaint. I'm protesting the misinterpretation of my views. Less so, I object to reading about the trustee action in the newspaper." He apologizes again for the lesser complaint.

The rest of our conversation was not so heated. Perhaps I missed an opportunity. What if I had invited them to understand what led me to my position? What if I had told them about Stan, Pat and Darrell, and the parents, Francis and Jim? They might have listened.

MAY 5, 1989

Jim Pitts, chaplain at Furman University in South Carolina, called today. "Now, don't worry but . . ." Of course, immediately I begin to worry.

He wants me to know that a protest movement led by Rev. Mac Greene is challenging the presence of Janice and me on the faculty of the Furman University's Pastor's School this summer. I don't know Mac Greene. According to Jim, he is a crusading South Carolina Baptist pastor who has found a holy cause in opposing my position on homosexuality. Once again, Janice is guilty by association.

Actually, Greene's target is Furman University, a state Baptist institution. For him, my invitation is a mere symptom of a liberal school that has veered away from its Christian moorings. I'm an easy enemy; homosexuality is the perfect hot button issue. Greene and his troops are applying pressure on the leadership of the South Carolina Baptist Convention to, in turn, strong arm Furman's leadership to dis-invite us.

It is interesting that our assignment at the Pastor's School has nothing to do with homosexuality. Marriage is the topic of our four lectures. But, as with Southeastern, the content of our lectures is not the issue. My presence illustrates the slippery slope of liberalism occurring at Furman.

Jim said not to worry, and I won't. This is his battle. It is a challenge to his leadership and, in some sense, to the leadership of Furman. Janice and I just may have an extra week of vacation this summer.

MAY 22, 1988

Jim Pitts called again. The Greene movement is gaining momentum. They have persuaded the executive of South Carolina convention to write Dr. Johns, president of Furman, requesting that I be removed from the faculty of the Pastor's School in July. His letter, signed also by the president, vice president, and Executive Committee chairman of the state convention, quotes extensively from the SBC Today article, concluding that "the good name of Furman University and the future of the Pastor's School are at stake."

MAY 26, 1989

Of all people, Mac Greene calls tonight.

He begins with an inviting voice, "Mahan, I realize that while I have been working to get you off of the Pastor's School's program this summer, I have never talked with you. Calling you directly is at least the Christian thing to do. Do you mind if I ask you a few questions? I want to be accurate in presenting your views on homosexuality." He proceeds with the typical litany, "Is it true that you believe . . .?"

I am hesitant. I don't trust him. Why would he wait until now to be so "Christian"? I tell him I am busy and would only talk with him for a few minutes. My responses to his questions are brief and general. My paranoia is on high alert.

What a strange place to be in. I'm the enemy, a threat to be stopped, a cancer to be cut out. I alternate between laughing and being anxious over my new role among some Baptists. I think of all the energy that Mac Greene is investing in this crusade. He is a pastor. Doesn't he have more important things to do?

But this is not about me, I have to keep reminding myself. It is about his agenda with Furman. He is using both me and the volatile fear of homosexuality in his bid for influence.

But here am I reading into the motives of others, the very thing I resent when I am the target. I don't know enough to read his mind. Neither does Greene know me. We both are standing up for our sense of right. Let it be, Mahan.

May 24, 1989

Jim tells us that the Furman board of trustees called a special meeting to consider the request from the state convention leadership to remove us from the Pastor's School's faculty. I find that amazing, busy trustees coming together to micromanage this problem.

Of course, their decision supports Jim. They are not about to interfere with the leadership of the Pastor's School. Yet they do allow Greene to rant and rail for almost an hour against my presence on the summer faculty. Is this comedy or tragedy? Both?

July 5, 1988

Here we are at the Furman Pastor's School. No protest. No hint of controversy. No mention of the Greene movement against our presence. Today is our first lecture on marriage, and well received, I think.

I credit the backing down of the resistance to clear stands taken first by Jim, then the board of trustees, and finally by Dr. Johns. Their firm "no" made the difference.

July 6, 1988

This afternoon Janice, Jim Pitts, and I met with Furman's president, Dr. Johns. Jim wants to demystify our threat to the university. He laughs, "Showing up with no horns protruding from your forehead might help." The meeting gives us a chance to thank Dr. Johns for his support and to thank Jim in the presence of the president.

Dr. Johns shares some information that caps the story of Mac Greene's phone call to me on the Sunday night in May. I had been cautious for good reason. Dr. Johns discovered that Greene's call was in fact a conference call. While Mac was asking his questions, other ministers were taking notes on my responses. The tactic backfired. It gave Dr. Johns a taste of their deviousness.

CHAPTER 4

Continuing Education

January, 1989–June, 1990

JANUARY 18, 1989

FOR SOME TIME NOW I have spoken of sexual "orientation," not sexual "preference."

"It is a watershed question," Bill boldly asserts in our RRNGLE meeting this morning. "Is sexual orientation chosen or discovered?" He continues, "Would I have chosen or preferred to be homosexual, knowing all the prejudice that comes with it? For most of my years, I assumed I was a perverted heterosexual. I knew, even as a boy of six or seven, that I was different from the other boys, but not until I was a freshman at State did I dare to name the truth. Gradually I acknowledged this part of myself."

While Bill is talking, I am nodding in agreement. Whether we discover or choose sexual orientation is a crucial question. If homosexuality is a preference chosen, then we can choose otherwise.

Then Rich speaks up, taking issue with Bill. "I am bisexual. I don't like the tight categories of homosexual and heterosexual. Some try to squeeze themselves into one or the other, like I did." As a gay man, Rich has been leading a support group for gay men who meet weekly at Pullen. Recently he introduced us to Barbara whom he plans to marry this spring.

Rich prefers Kinsey's continuum of sexuality: at opposite poles, some people are either exclusively homosexual or heterosexual in orientation, while others live somewhere in between, not completely one or the other. Rich sees himself in the middle of this continuum, experiencing sexual attraction toward both the same and the opposite sex. By now, I am scratching my head.

I think of Brenda. For eighteen years she was married to a man who periodically abused her. Now she seems happy in a committed relationship with another woman. I wonder: Is she bisexual or has she been lesbian all along? Perhaps she, like Darrell, married hoping that she could overcome her homosexuality. Or, she may have found at last a mature partner who offers her a life-giving relationship. Like Rich, she also defies neat categorization.

Have I looked for clarity about sexual orientation that doesn't exist? Am I, along with others, trying to superimpose a construct of sexuality that does not fit the complexities?

JANUARY 26, 1989

I am at the beach with our first RRNGLE retreat. Present are Morris, Nancy, Jim, Alan, Phyllis, Jimmy, Dave, Ted, and me. Six denominations represented. I look around our group and wonder what accounts for us spending this kind of time together.

Friendship, for one thing. The subject, the church and homosexuality has brought us together. If it weren't for RRNGLE, few of us would know each other. Along with the laughter and learning, the others in the group give me courage. Perhaps I would have offered my understanding of homosexuality to Pullen without RRNGLE. But I doubt I would have written articles and letters to the editor, walked in the Gay Pride March, or spoken for gay concerns in community meetings if it hadn't been for this network of collegial support.

JANUARY 27, 1989

I come to this retreat with the particular interest of hearing Jim Lewis, a former parish priest in West Virginia, discuss his rationale for conducting same-gender unions. It's only a matter of time before a gay couple will ask me to perform such a ceremony.

In this priestly ministry, Jim sees himself pronouncing God's blessing on covenant love no different in content from the blessing of heterosexual couples. One is legal and ecclesiastically proper, the other is not, but the inherent celebration of life-long, mutual commitment within the context of a faith community is the same. That makes good sense to me. Jim, and Jimmy as well, provide this ministry on their own without the sanction of their denominations—Episcopal in Jim's case and Methodist in Jimmy's case. It is for them an act of protest that is both prophetic and pastoral.

Being a Baptist, I cannot conceive of performing such a service unless the congregation adopts this ritual. Our differences in church polity are showing. When I speak and act, I represent this particular community of faith that elected me for pastoral leadership. This covenant, in my opinion, prohibits me from conducting a life transition rite on my own.

February 15, 1989

Another death from AIDS. Another funeral. They are happening more frequently now. As I'm finding is typical, present are lots of friends but few family members.

At Roy's funeral this afternoon, only his mother is present. The family rejection, except for his mother, deepens the pathos.

Yet Roy did not die without love. Present today and all during these past days is his partner, introduced by him as his "lover." His eight or so friends could not have been more attentive. Add to this "family" the four members of the AIDS Care Team. All of them were the faithful ones with Roy during his last weeks of erratic moods, swinging from delirious stupor to clarity of mind, back and forth, back and forth.

The usual categories don't work. I am accustomed to placing people in roles, such as husband and wife, mother and father, brother and sister, clergy and laity, Christian and non-Christian. To speak of Roy as gay and his friends as both gay and straight is to say so little of importance. Even the title "partner" is bland. Stripped of traditional categories, what stands out to me is the title "lover." The word "love" best describes the reality being celebrated in today's service.

I think of Roy's mother. She is going back to her small town in western North Carolina by herself. Will she be able to talk about Roy's funeral? Who will receive her anguish? Grief becomes manageable only when placed in a story. If so, who will listen to her story? Likely, the fact of Roy's sexuality and his death from AIDS will remain her guarded secret, her private heartbreak.

March 12, 1989

At our second RRNGLE conference, again held at Pullen, theologian Carter Heyward is our guest lecturer. She is strong, insightful and, yes, in keeping with the title of her recent book, she speaks with "passion for justice."

Her opening prayer set the tone of her presence:

Spirit of integrity, you drive us into the desert to search out our truths. Give us clarity to know what is right and courage to reject what is merely strategic, that we may abandon the false innocence of failing to choose at all.

Carter begins her lecture with her life's story. Reared in Charlotte in an upper class Episcopalian family, she played by the rules, winning "trophies" along the way. Then she broke ranks, first in her theological thinking, then in her ordination as a woman, and finally in "coming out" as a lesbian.

Her mother and brother came from Charlotte to be present with us. There is a homecoming feel to the entire event, for her and for us, especially evident in the closing worship experience. In new and profound ways, we are coming home to parts of ourselves, to each other, and in some instances, to God. Healing happened today.

For me Carter connects the dots. She helps me see that the struggle for lesbian and gay equality is one expression of the same ferment within all liberation movements whether racial, gender, or economic. Oppression at one point contributes to the oppression at every point. Freedom for some raises the level of freedom for all. Gay liberation is one expression of a larger longing for shalom.

Carter's closing challenge: "Our fear of our strength may be our undoing. And our learning to stand and speak up for ourselves may well be our salvation."

MARCH 13, 1989

Jon Walton, pastor of Westminster Presbyterian Church in Wilmington, Delaware, is the other speaker today. He's white, heterosexual, a husband, father and senior minister of a sizeable middle/upper class congregation. In other words, he is like me. He also has been converted by pastoral conversations with lesbians and gays. A kindred spirit.

MARCH 16, 1989

Charles was in the small group that I facilitated during the RRNGLE conference last weekend. He has lived with his partner for seventeen years, yet without the legal supports granted to heterosexual married couples.

Charles puts a face and words to the current reality: legal, social, often familial, and certainly religious systems work against gay couples sustaining committed relationships.

I take for granted the supports in my marriage. In contrast, Charles and his partner have few stakeholders in their relationship. Add to this, the church's sweeping judgement, "Gays engage in promiscuous life styles!" God, help us.

AUGUST 12, 1989

Mac comes to see me today. We have met before around church tasks. Not this time. He wants to talk about his daughter, Lillian.

He is apologetic. "Mahan, I feel bad about two things. One, maybe I'm a coward, but I cannot admit to anyone that my daughter is homosexual. And two, I feel I should support your efforts more openly, but I just can't."

He turns to his deeper anguish. "We have not been able to invite Lillian's partner to our family gatherings. I know that Lillian wants May to be included, but frankly it would threaten our pleasant times together. You know how different our children are, particularly when it comes to religion. Lillian and May's commitment of seven years makes a difference to me but not to our children. Patrick is so opposed to Lillian's relationship with May. Why, if she came with Lillian for Christmas, I wouldn't be surprised if Patrick and his family packed their bags and left."

Mostly I listen. Toward the end of our conversation, he adds: "Besides, to be honest, I am still sorting through my own responses to Lillian. It has only been a few years since she put words to what we had suspected. I want to be further along. Margie is, but I am not."

Mac and I know how to do church work together. He can analyze a church problem with wisdom I admire, but our time together today is different, more intimate. Courage marks his reaching out to me.

DECEMBER 7, 1989

Steve is devastated. He appears at my office door with none of his characteristic charisma, almost too shocked and embarrassed to talk even in the privacy of my office. In a low, measured voice he speaks of being terminated from his teaching position at St. Phillips. It seems that two colleagues in this private high school were involved in a homosexual affair, and Steve is mentioned in one of their letters.

I don't know any further details. With Steve's permission, I call Dick, a lawyer in the church always willing to assist when legal counsel is needed. He will look into it and represent Steve's best interests.

Steve appears utterly demolished—his fulfilling career over, his friendships severed, his marriage damaged. His life is over, he feels, so much so, that I ask for a promise. "If you begin obsessing about suicide, call me night or day." He says he would.

DECEMBER 8, 1989

I saw Steve again today. Taking his own life remains an appealing option. Death would offer relief from the embarrassment and perhaps the guilt. Only one obstacle prevents him from self-destruction. Suicide would magnify the pain felt by Denise and the children. His concern for them is keeping him in this world.

If homosexuality was not involved, would there have been more care in the school's response? His superiors performed emergency surgery, cutting him from the school like a malignant cancer. In fairness, some friends have reached out to Steve, but his shame prohibits a response. He doesn't feel worthy of friendship. He is embarrassed to death.

DECEMBER 31, 1989

Steve is stumbling into 1990 with no goals, no community, no wishes, it seems, except death. His faith in God is shattered, leaving a profound sense of God's absence. Before he left the office today, we prayed Psalm 13, noting particularly the words—How long must I bear pain in my soul, and have sorrow in my heart all day long?"

JANUARY 9, 1990

Just when I think I am clear about homosexuality, something happens to topple my certainties. Kathy's challenge pulls me back into the mystery that human sexuality is.

"While I appreciate your stand, I take issue with you at one point," she says. "I question your conviction that one's sexual orientation is discovered, not chosen. This is not always true. Take me, for instance. I was in a committed relationship with another woman for eight years. We broke up several years ago. Now, I find myself strongly attracted to a man. We are dating. It might lead to marriage."

"You are not the first to challenge me about this point," I admit. "I've met a few people who don't fit into the set categories of sexual orientation."

"Well, I am one. It might have more to do with finding a mature, mutual love that includes physical, intellectual, spiritual and emotional intimacy. Maybe for most people a particular sexual orientation is the way they are constituted, but for me, these labels are rigid and restrictive."

FEBRUARY 1, 1990

Had lunch with Roger today. From a distance, I have admired him and his ministry in South Carolina. For years he has been a respected leader in his denomination. I had no idea why he requested a time together.

He wants to talk about Gerald who "came out" to Roger and his wife a few months ago. Gerald is the older of two sons and currently midway through his seminary studies. Roger has good reasons for anxiety—worry for Gerald and his vocational future, concern about his wife, and fear for his job. "I would lose my church if they know about Gerald," he laments.

But, to his credit, his concern focuses on Gerald. "Is this a phase? Can he change? Do you think he is naïve, believing he can be gay and be a minister?"

Roger is not looking for answers so much as a safe place to talk. "I have never thought much about homosexuality. I wondered if I would ever face this issue in the church, but never dreamed of confronting this in my family."

When I volunteer to meet with his wife, he shakes his head, "No, not for now anyway. Maybe later. She is confused and needs time."

I commend him for wanting to maintain a relationship with his son and work toward understanding. I recommend James Nelson's *Embodiment* and *Is the Homosexual My Neighbor?* by Mollenkott and Scanzoni. We agree to meet again.

MARCH 11, 1990

This weekend marks our third RRNGLE annual conference, again at Pullen. George Edwards, our lecturer this year, is a soft-spoken, hard hitting, poetic scholar and former professor of New Testament at Louisville Presbyterian Seminary.

In his opening comments he sets the theme and tone of his message. The proof-text use of scripture against homosexuality is "a product of fundamentalist indoctrination against which education must continually strive, if tradition and creed are not to overwhelm the redemptive power of religion and drive the central dynamic of our biblical legacy into a new kind of Babylonian captivity."

He encourages us to "allow meanings of scripture operating at frequencies hidden to earlier ears to break forth with undreamed importance." I think of the biblical concept of covenant. For me it is "breaking forth with undreamed importance" when related to same-gender commitments.

MARCH 22, 1990

This morning theologian Marjorie Suchocki lectured on the topic of original sin from a process perspective. Without referring to homosexuality specifically, she helps me think theologically about the church's response to gays.

We are born, Suchocki asserts, into systems (cultural, economic, social, political and religious) that work to the well being of some and to the detriment of others. The fear of homosexuality and the dominant power of heterosexuals, for instance, are part of the climate into which we are born. Heterosexuals are privileged; homosexuals are not.

No one taught me that homosexual men are deviant, queer, and always on the prowl. I don't remember a conversation about lesbians being men-haters. However, those messages were and are internalized. I inhaled these prejudices from the East Tennessee air of my childhood. In high school I relished the in-group feeling from ridiculing homosexuals. This is original sin, according to Suchocki. I have inherited, embodied, and benefited from these social disparities.

According to her schema, the first step toward transformation is awareness. Confession acknowledges our complicity with these unequal, unfair arrangements. By taking seriously our participation in evil, in this instance homophobia, we can turn [repent] toward just behavior. Our privileges need not, and in fact cannot be denied. However, they can become leverage in the service of just relationships.

MARCH 23, 1990

Margaret was also attending the Suchocki lectures. I haven't seen her since Winston-Salem days. Catching up on our families quickly gave way to her personal challenge. "They can change," she insists. "Gays choose to be homosexual. They can choose otherwise, especially if they turn their lives over to Christ!" She obviously knows about my gay advocacy.

I ask her if she knows anybody who has changed from one sexual orientation to another. She doesn't but she has read of such accounts from writers she trusts.

With Margaret so adamant about change, I thought about Rick, a recent referral. Rick began his visit telling me that I am the first heterosexual to hear that he is gay. Then he proceeds to chronicle all of his efforts to change. He tried the dating scene, but the sexual attraction toward girls, so strong in his friends, was not in him. He experienced kissing. It repulsed him. "What's wrong with my wiring?" he kept asking himself.

Next, he speaks of turning to God. Surely, God would change him and make him normal. Nothing happened. God, as far as he could tell, doesn't care. Of late, he has prayed that God would take him. He is tired of the struggle, weary of the shame and loneliness.

After relaying the story of Rick to Margaret, I add: "I don't know that a person's sexuality cannot be changed. My reading does not support that possibility, but mostly, I am influenced by the stories I have heard, like Rick's."

I suggest to Margaret that we are discussing a mystery that neither of us understands completely.

June 5, 1990

Today's event for Jimmy Creech is bittersweet, both sad and joyous at the same time. His friends met at the Methodist building to celebrate his ministry at Fairmont and grieve over its discontinuance. We had hoped for his re-appointment.

A number of us offer brief comments. "His prophetic voice that we lift up today," I suggest, "comes from the passion of a pastor. Jimmy is a pastor who speaks out loud the pain he experiences in pastoral conversations."

Bill Brantley is present also. Just ten days ago I sat beside him at Raleigh's first showing of the AIDS quilt at the Convention Center. We both were invited to say a few words at this emotionally charged event. In the few minutes before our talks, we introduced ourselves to each other, quickly discovering mutual friends.

Then today at Jimmy's event, here is Bill again. He comes in late and claims the seat next to me, the only vacant one in the chapel. After the service I turn to him; "This is twice in a few days when we have landed side by side. I think it is intended that you and I get acquainted. Let's have lunch soon."

JUNE 12, 1990

Lunched with Bill Brantley today. He's bright, self-assured, knowledgeable, and talkative. Our common age and shared concerns work for a quick, easy connection. He was married for twenty-eight years, has three boys, is a former journalist and political campaigner, and finally a businessman in the '60s and '70s. Though currently an Episcopalian, Bill grew up a Baptist and remains current about our denominational struggles against the fundamentalist push for biblical inerrancy.

Bill discovered he had AIDS in 1984. Already he has outlived many younger men with AIDS for whom he has been a mentor. Bill is an activist, investing his mind, energy, and voice in a just and compassionate response to others living with AIDS. He is estranged from his wife, cut off from two of his boys, and loosely connected with the other one. Only his Aunt Margaret is fully supportive. The contrast is poignant: estranged from his young adult sons, yet surrogate father to many young adults with AIDS.

We talk for over two hours. I come from our lunch knowing that a strong friendship is in the making. He's on a mission, as eager to teach me as I am to learn. And he is looking for a pastor, I think.

JUNE 13, 1990

Bill Brantley is a guest tonight at our house gathering. I had explained to Bill that my wife Janice and I have eight young adults living in our home and that every two weeks we have a meal together. Tonight is my time for the program, so I invited Bill.

Bill astonishes everyone, including me, with his level of self-revelation. "What an enormous relief to be honest," he says to his curious listeners giving rapt attention to each word. "I was dishonest with others and myself for so long. You can't know the burden! Now—it's a gift from my AIDS— I don't have time not to speak truth."

Bill proceeds to talk openly. He married, he says, hoping he would change. "I was a 'queer' and thought, like so many men my age, that a woman would bring out the heterosexual in me. Well, she didn't. For all of those years I kept my secret and lived at times a hidden life. I hated it. No, . . . I hated me." Bill keeps talking with no hint of boredom or disinterest around the table. He seems to anticipate the questions we did not know to ask. He is obviously delighted by a group of young adults fascinated by his story.

As is our custom, we close the evening with a Service of Communion. We remain around the table as Janice lights the candles and places a leftover roll on a plate. I pour the wine. Often this familiar rite feels like a seamless part of the meal and discussion, symbolizing the communion that graces our evening together. It did tonight.

JUNE 30, 1990

As the new convener of RRNGLE, I was invited to preach today at the Chapel of the Cross in Chapel Hill. A religious service is always part of the annual Gay Pride March. The chapel is full, mostly of gay men and lesbians. I am unprepared for the charged atmosphere. These waves of energy, I assume, arise from the shared pathos of pain and mutual yearning for community. I've heard leaders of worship talk about those occasional times when they are carried along by the spirit of a worshipping congregation. This is one of those times for me.

I can only guess the elements that came together with unusual force. The *place:* a small, traditional, beautifully appointed Episcopal chapel; the *setting:* a closing event of a march of protest and pride amid the backdrop of hostile voices; the *people:* a congregation full of persons, unashamed of their sexuality and spirituality; the *rituals:* treasures of song, symbol and story from a Christian tradition known for gay rejection; and me: a *heterosexual pastor,* a Baptist declaring good news, not condemnation. This uncommon convergence released in us profound joy.

CHAPTER 5

Pullen Going Public

July 5, 1990–June 28, 1991

JULY 5, 1990

A QUESTION RAISES THE ANTE WITH the sixteen deacons who gathered in the Griffin parlor tonight. Is it time to move toward an explicit welcome of gays at Pullen? Pat Levi, deacon chair, thinks it is. So do Pat Long and I.

Pat Long came to the deacons' meeting with a proposal: She suggests that we begin a conversation within the congregation about homosexuality. She offers a process patterned after a Methodist program for Reconciling Congregations. Each deacon had been sent a copy of this information.

The deacons quickly sense the difference this would make at Pullen. The issue of homosexuality would be no longer "out there," a topic that I might address occasionally in the pulpit or on printed page. No longer would Pullen's involvement be limited to the use of our church building for annual RRNGLE conferences. No: if they approved Pat's proposal, more members would be directly engaged, moving the topic from the margins of Pullen toward the center.

They want time to consider the implications of going down this path. Wisely, I think, the deacons postpone a decision until the August meeting.

As a part of her presentation, Pat Long takes a risk. "Many of you have known me for eleven years. You know me as a choir member, a liturgist, a community outreach worker, a friend." Then she told them about the impact of my sermon last June, the one that included my response to her anonymous letter. In that sermon she heard God's deep, loving, unconditional acceptance. "It's important," she concludes, "for the church to address this issue, to let us be whole people, to let us hear the gospel. Many gay and lesbian Christians have never heard the good news of God's acceptance."

In her self-revealing Pat reframes the deacon discussion. Homosexuality ceases to be a topic of study for the congregation. Now we are considering a study about our relationship with Pat and others like her. We all leave knowing that something significant has happened tonight.

AUGUST 4, 1990

Tonight, with eyes wide open, the deacons take a next step. The twenty leaders came together anticipating a far-reaching decision. In the discussion about Pat's proposal from last month's meeting, the opinions range from "This is not the time" to "It's time to adopt a clear statement of gay acceptance."

After extensive discussion, the deacons decide to authorize a church conversation with no expectation of outcome. "Let's proceed with an open forum for educational purposes, and see what happens." They are unwilling to project an eventual congregational decision.

The deacons put their finger on a critical issue: I do have a hope in mind. I hope the church will eventually take a clear welcoming stance, and I want this open discussion to be the next step in that direction. But I hope, as well, for a respectful process that will reflect the collective will of the congregation. For that to occur I cannot, nor can other leaders, be attached to a particular outcome.

So how do we embark upon this process without it being experienced as a means to a specific end?

This is the leadership challenge: Can we invite and structure authentic dialogue that educates without coercing, that invites change without willing a change already assumed? Can we who bring convictions to this conversation still be open to the truth in differing voices?

SEPTEMBER 15, 1990

Pat Long's article in this week's *Pullenews* is excellent. The content is balanced. The tone is welcoming. Her title, "Pullen and Homosexuality: An Invitation," introduces the open forum on homosexuality scheduled to begin Sunday evening, October 7.

It begins: "Whatever you believe about homosexuality, some part of the Christian community agrees with you." She proceeds to demonstrate the diverse convictions of the various religious traditions.

Her questions anticipate the exploration to which the congregation is invited:

How do we deal with a painful and emotionally charged issue in ways that bring mutual healing rather than alienation and division? What does it mean to be lesbian or gay? Is it a choice or a given, defect or variation, sin or gift? What does the Bible say—and not say—about homosexuality? In what contexts was it written? How can we create a safe space where confidentiality is respected and honesty is possible? How do we move beyond debating theory to understanding human experience? How can we deal responsibly with the moral issues involved? What would it mean for our congregation to be an agent of reconciliation between the church and the gay community? How can we offer gays and lesbians the liberation of openness without threatening for others the legitimate need to remain private? Where is the pain in our own community? How can we respect the diversity of feelings and beliefs among us so that genuine dialogue is possible? What does it mean to be faithful to God in this context?

Her closing words: "The task we undertake is a difficult one, but the possibilities are life-transforming."

September 29, 1990

The worship service this morning is a *wonderful disaster.* Only this paradoxical description does it justice.

One theme of the service is our church's response to the AIDS crisis. I invited Jimmy Creech to preach and Bill Brantley to give the four-minute Focus we often include in our worship services.

The *disaster* part? The intended four-minute Focus becomes the sermon, leaving Jimmy with little time and depleted congregational energy. The sermon is anti-climatic.

It is my fault, totally my mistake. Bill limited to four minutes? He couldn't be limited to four minutes about any subject, especially his experience as a person living with AIDS. The four minutes becomes forty minutes, wreaking havoc with our neatly designed order of worship. This isn't fair to Bill and certainly not to Jimmy.

But here is the *wonderful* part. Bill is the first person to talk openly as a gay man from the lectern or pulpit at Pullen. As if that is not a sufficient shock, add that he is a person with AIDS. Bill speaks about himself with breathtaking honesty and openness. Most members, probably nine out of ten, have never heard a story like Bill's. To think that he could or should be held to four minutes!

Bill talks with the freedom of a person who has come to grips with his own dying. He says this morning what I have heard him say privately: he gives thanks for his life with AIDS. "If it weren't for my disease, I would not know what really matters—integrity, friends, and God."

Something shifted today in the congregation and within him as well. We all are thrown off balance. The cracks in our clockwork service became openings for fresh air, for Spirit. It was a wonderful disaster.

OCTOBER 7, 1990

In tonight's first Open Forum on Homosexuality and the Church, Pullen crosses another threshold. The Forum marks the movement from pulpit to pew, from preacher to laity, from monologue to dialogue. The stakes are higher. The outcomes are less controllable.

About fifty persons are present, including at least thirty Pullen members who represent a cross section of the congregation. The rest of the group are strangers to me. Word about the event had obviously spread around the community.

We form one large circle. By joining hands, seeing faces, and hearing words of welcome, our anxiety is lowered a notch or two. Those from Pullen know the importance of our gathering. Those from the community are anxious for other reasons. They risk coming into a group of unfamiliar faces, church people no less.

Next, Pat and I tell our personal stories, describing the paths that led us to this place of open forum. This too reduces the tension. Most everyone could identify with parts of our narratives.

Then each person is given three blank cards on which to list fears, questions, and suggestions. Later Pat and I read aloud from these unsigned cards. The questions are recorded on newsprint and become the basis for future Forum meetings. Pat is taking the lead, along with a steering committee soon to be formed.

OCTOBER 20, 1990

Chris thought I could help. "The next time my parents visit, talk to them.

I have told them I am gay, but they never want to discuss it."

After the service this morning, Chris ushers his parents back to my office. Then he exits with a "make it all right" kind of glance in my direction. His parents are from rural North Carolina, active in their church, and obviously proud of Chris.

Quickly into our conversation Chris's mother states their position: "Chris told us he is homosexual about a year ago. We don't understand it but don't care to talk about it. Chris wants to but we don't. Chris continues to be the sweet boy he has always been. That's what matters. We love it when he comes home. His nieces and nephews adore him. Now, if he brings home a male friend, someone he is living with, that's another matter. We can't handle that."

Then she speaks more directly to me. "Chris has been pushing us to talk with you. I know you must be a fine man and you have been good to him. We appreciate that, but we don't want to talk about homosexuality. It's so unnatural. Our preacher says he will get over it. Someday he'll find the right girl and settle down."

My cautious attempt to offer another perspective receives no response. Then I move the conversation to Chris and his contributions to Pullen. They smile with a parent's pride. "Someday," I suggest, "you may want to discuss Chris's homosexuality. If so, perhaps I can be helpful."

Chris is disappointed. He hoped for more.

OCTOBER 27, 1990

Even though attendance is optional and publicity minimal, the Open Forum's existence is causing a stir. Some members are objecting to any public reference. They particularly object to notices being listed in the worship bulletins and newsletter as one of the educational opportunities. "Why can't you list the event as 'Open Forum,' and leave out 'on Homosexuality'?"

Up to this point I have not spoken or written publicly about the Open Forum. I feel it's time to do so. My article in the newsletter includes these words:

Some of you have expressed concern. I have concern as well. Please read carefully my comments. Even daring to discuss openly this subject as a congregation is to open ourselves to volatile, divisive possibilities.

Our Pullen commitment to mutual respect and understanding, values we so highly prize, will be stretched to the fullest, because complexity, ignorance, fear, honest differences, and mystery cling like barnacles to this issue. But homosexuality is not an issue. Homosexuality, like heterosexuality, is about people . . . these people are us, our family members, our friends and neighbors. At Pullen we are involved, whether we face that or not. So is every other church, whether they know it or not.

A few congregations choose to condemn and stereotype. Most Christian leadership chooses to deny and avoid. But there is such resulting confusion, anger, fear, and self-deprecation, we must, for God's sake, seek the ways of compassion. We, at Pullen, are attempting to provide a place of healing and understanding . . . .

The Forum . . . [is] a gathering place for persons of whatever sexual orientation to pursue the connection of spirituality and sexuality through questions, Bible study, and shared insight. The aim is education, not agreement; understanding, not coercion. I am hoping all points of view can be heard and respected . . . .

We are in the midst of a revolution . . . I am proud that we, as a congregation, are willing to face, learn from, [and] grow from this major challenge and opportunity of our time.

OCTOBER 30, 1990

Steve died this morning. The beginning of his end started last December when he was dismissed for being implicated in a homosexual affair between two other teachers. The end came today. Finally, his wish is granted, I thought as I hung up the phone.

Steve never recovered from the loss of position, loss of pride, and in the deepest sense, loss of self. His shame, so close to the surface, sabotaged every new start with his life. He and I worked together on a few projects, but there was no fire within him. He tried. He blew on the embers, but no flame returned. In late September, his wish came true. The diagnosis of inoperable cancer brought relief, not despair. At last, his embarrassment is mercifully lifted.

Yesterday Denise, children Alice and Richard, and I encircled Steve's bed, searching for and finding the words of gratitude, regret and good-bye. Truly, it was a circle of mercy. Peace, at last for Steve.

MARCH 11, 1991

The Forum is having limited educational impact on the congregation. With few exceptions only those who are affected directly with the concerns around homosexuality are attending. Only a few congregational leaders are present.

I understand the small response to the Forum. Why expose yourself to such an unsettling unfamiliar topic? When you are already living close to the edge, trying to make do with multiple stresses, why open the door to unanswered questions with people, most of whom are strangers?

I understand because I was in that same category. I did not pursue this injustice. It came to me. Homosexuality became the faces of people who crossed my path, came into my life, and, more to the point, invited me into their lives. Why should I be surprised that limited numbers are participating in the Open Forum?

MARCH 20, 1991

Lee wants to be baptized this Easter. I am thrilled. There are others also preparing for this public commitment, but Lee is the pleasant surprise.

We first met last fall. He is early for his appointment, as I recall. I open the door, welcome Lee, and suggest he take the chair opposite me. Sitting on its edge, his body announces ambivalence: "I want to be here; I'm scared to be here!"

"My sister tells me I am going to hell. Am I?" he blurts out. "I have been with my partner, James, for eleven years. We've been faithful to each other all these years, but that makes no difference to her."

Lee relaxes slightly and continues, "Just before I left home, I was talking with my sister. She blew a gasket when I told her I was coming to talk with the pastor at Pullen Memorial in Raleigh. 'Don't you know that man is a blasphemer! That church is evil! Lee, the truth is clear. Homosexuality is an abomination to God. You are living in sin. Your years with James do not change a thing. Unless you repent you are going to hell.'"

What power he grants his sister, I'm thinking. Her voice carries such authority in his life. He makes that very point. "Every time I talk with her, she stirs up my fears. Usually I am okay. But when she talks, she seems so sure, reminding me that the scriptures are absolutely clear. I never know what to say."

I am in that pastoral place again, up against inner, compelling voices that shout down any affirming word. With my strongest voice I declare the counter word of God's love for him, a grace no less because of his homosexuality. And I commend his life with James. "Your sister may not look with favor on your faithful relationship with James. I do, and I believe God does."

Lee left my office that day eager to test this other voice of acceptance. And he has. For these months his curiosity and hunger seem insatiable. He has been consistently in our worship services and educational events, engaging members in conversation about their faith, reading and studying. He can't seem to get enough.

And today he is asking for baptism. Too soon? Maybe, but I don't think so. I know, in time, the ardor of his spiritual sprints will settle into the steadier pace of a long race. This next stage in his discipleship will come soon enough. Why not baptism, I say. In one sense, he has already taken the plunge. He's immersed. It's happening. His baptism would make public and communal what is obviously occurring privately.

MARCH 25, 1991

At last, I have found a biblical passage that supports the welcome of gays into the church.

Yesterday, while driving to Winston-Salem, I was listening to Bishop Spong debate another bishop from Florida about the church and homosexuality. Spong mentions a reference from Acts in passing. I find the passage compelling.

The story of Cornelius' conversion in Acts 10 turns out to be Simon Peter's conversion as well. And its connection with the Jerusalem Council in Acts 15 offers a parallel to the church's response to gays in our day. Cornelius is a Gentile, unclean in the eyes of any faithful Jew, including Simon Peter. Plus, as a Roman centurion, he embodies the oppression of Rome. On two accounts, he is a threat to the Jewish community.

Yet much to Peter's surprise Cornelius shares his love of God. His devotion is evident. The message to Peter is startling but undeniable: God shows no partiality. Not only Jews but Gentiles, like Cornelius, are being inflamed by the Holy Spirit.

So, Peter, loyal to his tradition, goes to the leaders of the church in Jerusalem with the evidence. God is clearly embracing Gentiles, like

Cornelius. With them Peter raises the question: "Can anyone withhold the water for baptizing these people who have received the Holy Spirit just as we have?" After much discussion, "No," is the decision by the Jewish leaders in Jerusalem. "We must not restrict the clear work of the Spirit."

According to his reading of the Torah, the Bible, Peter sees no basis for the unqualified inclusion of the Gentiles. Both his tradition, and, likely, his visceral responses, declare Gentiles as unclean. But his dream in Joppa dramatizes the conversion required of him and other Jewish leaders. They must learn to see with God's eyes. What they are calling unclean, God regards as clean and worthy.

The parallel seems obvious to me. Our tradition, our Torah (Bible) and, often our visceral responses declare homosexuals as unclean. I hear this regularly: "The Bible says that homosexuality is a sin. Just show me where the scriptures support gays or lesbians." And I can't. I cannot reference any clear affirmation of homosexuals in the scriptures.

Yet, with Peter, I cannot deny what the Spirit is doing. I experience the evidence of God's grace in many gays and lesbians. I know their faith. I see their courage. I stand amazed before their patience with a church so reluctant to welcome their commitment. We, who are participants in the Jesus movement in our time, are being stretched beyond our comfort zone no less than Peter was stretched beyond his.

MAY 9, 1991

Tonight's experience is an investment in memory. I won't forget it. Jim Lewis, Jimmy Creech, and I were invited to address the gay men's business club.

First of all, I did not know there is such a thing as a gay men's business club. At least 125 are present. The climate in the room feels emotionally charged from the moment we are seated at the head table. I'm guessing it is a mixture of hostility and curiosity, hostility against the church and curiosity about our presence. As clergy, we represent the major institution that has consistently condemned them through the years.

Up front, at the beginning of our comments, each one of us acknowledges the sins of the church. We do not sidestep their rejection through church history, reflected in gay bashing still prominent in our day. We confess, as well, the covert behavior of the church by looking the other way when violence against homosexuals occurs. Then we tell our personal history with homosexuality, particularly highlighting people, like themselves, who are changing us with their life stories.

At that point the mood calms considerably. The ground beneath us feels more level and the open discussion that follows is lively, full of comments and questions, spiced with laughter. I detect a wistfulness among them. I hear this in the one who expressed the dilemma: I both resent and miss the church. Another person asks if there are congregations that welcome gays. At this point Tim, one of the few I know, stands up and invites the questioner to Pullen. "You will be welcome there," he said. A proud moment for me.

May 11, 1991

The experience with the gay business club last night has stayed with me in a dark way. The exuberance in last night's journal entry has evaporated. Anger is what I feel today.

I'm remembering a room full of responsible, contributing citizens. Yet they are deemed unworthy and unacceptable to most churches and civic groups. If they were open about their sexual orientation, they would not likely be welcomed into Rotary, Kiwanis, or 95 percent of congregations. Their need to meet separately as a business club is a judgment upon us all.

June 16, 1991

Gary, a Protestant minister from a nearby town, came to see me this morning. He reminds me of Darrell, the Presbyterian layman who came a year or so ago. His opening words are essentially the same: "I want another human being to know the truth about me. I'm not asking for counseling, and don't intend to come back."

He tells me his story. He has three young children, cares for his wife and loves his work. He hoped that marriage, parenting and church ministry would control, if not supplant his homosexual fantasies. They have not.

From the outside, people assume that he enjoys a fulfilling life. From the inside, he daily fights the fear that his sexual desires cannot be contained or, fear of all fears, his secret will be discovered. No one knows the truth, not even his wife, unless she knows but remains silent. They have never addressed the issue.

I offer more times to get together. "If not with me, there are therapists that would provide a safe place for you and your wife to talk. Consider doing for yourself what you would likely recommend to a parishioner."

But he is adamant. He wants only this time with me, another man, another minister, another human ear. He is not willing to talk further. He did request prayer.

I'm reminded again of the underworld out there. How many others harbor these secrets?

CHAPTER 6

The Gathering Storm

August 18, 1991–January 7, 1992

AUGUST 18, 1991

IT'S BEEN A YEAR NOW. The leaders of the Open Forum on Homosexuality authorized by the deacons last August met tonight to plan for the future. I have been on the margins, attending the meetings occasionally. From my perspective, the Forum has accomplished three things: It has provided a safe place for learning; a close-knit community of about thirty has formed because of it; and, by the regular announcements of its meetings, the entire congregation has been reminded that this conversation is occurring among us.

In June, Mark Smith, along with some Forum participants, reported to the deacons about their first year. Then in July, Jim Powell, the new chair, presented to the deacons a list of committees, including a committee to explore being an inclusive congregation.

AUGUST 28, 1991

I hear the argument:"Why bother to make explicit our inclusion of gays and lesbians? They *are* welcome. They are vital members. Some are leaders, like Pat Long who was just elected a deacon. Gay acceptance among us is happening. Why begin a discussion in the congregation that will only stir things up?"

This is my answer: Naming makes a difference. I remember the first time I told Janice "I love you." The reality was already present, but when I named my love, the relationship took on an added dimension. If the reality is absent, then, of course, the naming is empty. The naming of love in a friendship is equally transforming. There is power released when word, as symbol, intersects with experience. I want us to give words to our increasing welcome of gay Christians. There is power in naming.

SEPTEMBER 12, 1991

I have said for a couple of years that someday a couple, either two men or two women, would request the church's blessing upon their union. I had no idea about whom or when or how. Today is the day. The "who," "when" and "how" happened.

Eric Matthews and Ron Daniels make that request this morning. I had met Ron before. He is a member of nearby Methodist church, a friend of Jimmy Creech. Since Jimmy's exit he has been attending worship at Pullen. Eric is doing doctoral studies at NC State, has been a steady member of Pullen for about three years. In our limited times together, I experience him as shy, serious, and witty.

Eric takes the lead. They want the same support from their faith community, friends, and family that heterosexuals receive at their weddings. "We have been partners for almost three years. The idea of a ritual of blessing was raised in one of the Open Forum discussions. Since then we have talked about the possibility."

"Why the church?" I ask them. "You can have a ritual performed outside of the church with far less complication. You could still have your supportive friends and family members present." No, they want a church ceremony, and specifically a Pullen service, if possible. That's why they are coming first to me.

Eric and Ron don't know what they are asking, not completely. In their minds, their request is simple and straightforward, and in some sense it is. Their essential point is compelling. Relationships are tough to do well. Being gay in our society makes them even harder. They assume that a public ceremony that includes the important people in their lives will add a level of strength to their commitment.

I pick up no sense of protest or demand in their voices. Eric and Ron represent themselves, not the cause of gay rights. Pullen is their first choice. If a covenant service is not possible here, they will seek a more private ceremony outside of the church.

"This is not my decision to make," I explain. "The church must decide. I don't have the authority to conduct a public, precedent-setting ritual that has not been adopted by the congregation."

Eric, a Baptist, sees both sides: understanding the need for the congregation's affirmation and appreciating the congregation's freedom to do so. Ron seems puzzled, but takes heart in the possibility.

They leave sobered by the complexity of their request. They hadn't expected the three or four sessions for exploring the meaning and implications of their ceremony. Neither did they reckon on a process of decision-making that would include the deacons and perhaps the congregation. If they expected a clear "yes" or "no" today, they are disappointed.

Janice is spraying the roses in the back yard when I come home for supper. I greet her with ominous words: "Well, I am faced with what may be the most important decision of my ministry." I proceed to tell her about Eric and Ron's request. With no hint of alarm, she removes her gloves, lays down the hose and suggests we go inside to talk.

September 21, 1991

In my second meeting with Eric and Ron this morning, we begin where we left off in the last visit, the complexity of their request. Eric asks, "Why would this ceremony with friends and family be a threat to the church? No one will be forced to attend. Besides, there are other gay couples that attend Pullen, like Mason and Gene."

Ron is "closeted" at work. He would not dare tell those at work about his plans. Eric has a few colleagues that would be accepting. Neither one anticipates much excitement from his family. "But the church is different, or should be," Eric adds. "We have good friends here."

"Maybe the church can stand with you," I respond somewhat defensively. "I hope so, but understand that you are asking for a ceremony never before experienced in this congregation, nor in almost every other congregation, including two thousand years of church history. We have evidence of a few but not many same-gender ceremonies. Officiating at such a service would be a new venture for 99 percent of the pastors, including me. We may call it a 'blessing' of your covenant, but most people will hear in our words 'wedding' and 'marriage.' This will strike most people as unimaginable."

Most of our session focuses on their relationship—as I do with heterosexual couples preparing for marriage: communication patterns, particularly the handling of anger and conflict; the place of faith in their relationship; their relationships with their own families of origin; and their hopes for each other and their life together.

During this conversation, I feel the strangeness of new territory. They do as well. I'm exploring with them the same relational and intimacy issues I would with a heterosexual couple. All three of us are marching beyond familiar maps.

SEPTEMBER 22, 1991

Soon I must decide about Eric and Ron. We have talked enough for me to believe in the genuineness of their request to make covenant with each other within a service of worship. They are more ready than many couples. Some couples regard the wedding ceremony as a hurdle to jump over, not a ritual for faith expression and community participation. Not so with them.

Yet, they are gay. They want God's blessing and ours upon their union. That's history making. The implications for them, for the congregation, and for me are beyond measure. If I proceed to the deacons, we all may be profoundly affected in ways I cannot anticipate. I feel the pressure to decide building within me.

SEPTEMBER 28, 1991

Ron and Eric are solemn today. The naïveté I first experienced from them has modified. They didn't expect their request to be so challenging. For Eric especially, the uncertainties have only fueled his resolve. They have become more motivated, not less.

I delineate three realities: one, the length of time; two, the potential of public controversy; and three, the uncertainty of a positive response. Each one of these would be frustrating; together, they could be overwhelming.

Even if the deacons affirm their request, the process of decision-making by the congregation could take many months. Members, I explain, will need ample time to explore a very daunting recommendation. Then there is the media, I add. We cannot predict what the media will do with this unorthodox request.

I test them: "Are you prepared to go through this uncertainty and exposure?" Both quickly responded, "Yes."

But they are in the same position I am. We don't know what will happen, so how can we be fully prepared? We are moving into uncharted territory, particularly for Baptists. I told them that Jim Lewis and Jimmy Creech officiate at private holy union services, and the Unitarian Universalist congregations offer rituals for gay unions. But I don't know of any church, Baptist or not, that has faced this decision *as a congregation*.

There is no one to call up and ask, "How did you decide when to take this before your leadership? What happened when . . .? What did you do when . . .? How would you do it differently?" There is no congregational leader to call. There are no benchmarks to follow.

I finally catch myself. The conversation in my head and with them is coming from my anxiety, not theirs. I return to them, bringing our conversation to a close: "You have been clear about your desire and have been open with me in probing its meaning. Now, I must explore further my own response. I am ready to affirm your covenant to each other. I think it is the right thing to support. That's a pastoral response. But I am also a leader of Pullen. I must weigh the impact on the congregation."

My need for more time disappoints them. After four hours of conversation, they expected a ready "yes." I assure them that I am inclined to proceed but want to be sure.

OCTOBER 2, 1991

I'm preoccupied these days. This morning I am trying to write Sunday's sermon but cannot stay focused.

I worry about the congregation. A few weeks ago we were stymied. Pat and the leaders of the Forum, plus Jim and I, did not know what next steps to take. How could we move toward the consideration of a clear, open welcome to gays and lesbians?

Then, Ron and Eric appear out of the blue, a next step for sure! But is it too big a step? We were thinking of a statement of gay affirmation. Now, I am thinking of supporting, not only homosexual persons, but the blessing of gay unions. A huge stretch!

My anxiety is sky high, so intense I can't distinguish between a legitimate concern for Eric, Ron, the congregation and my insecurities at play. Where is my ego in this? Would stepping back and waiting be an act of cowardice or wisdom? Where is God in this? How can I tease apart my motivations?

OCTOBER 11, 1991

My annual trek with Ted Purcell in the mountains has come just in time. This year our section of the Appalachian Trail is from Mt. Rogers to Damascus, Virginia. Hiking grants me distance, both geographical and emotional distance. Perspective, too. The mountains invite the long view.

Of course, "the request" has come along on the trek. It's closer than the bottled water on my hip and trail food on my back. It clings like a soaking tee-shirt. The questions are more honed now: Is this the time to proceed with a process of decision-making of this magnitude?

Are the deacons, including perhaps the congregation, at stable places with sufficient strength for a fresh challenge? Are lay and staff leaders working well together? Will Pullen's history of seeking justice "kick in" and help stabilize us if we proceed with this risk?

This afternoon, while obsessing about these questions, suddenly a new question erupts: *Why am I trying to answer all of these questions alone? Aren't the deacons elected to oversee and clarify our mission?* Of course they are. These are *their* questions to answer along with me. Here am I trying to decide in advance what the church can or should do.

What a relief to see this.

OCTOBER 14, 1991

Today is our last day of hiking. I'm still feeling release from the earlier insight. The readiness of the church and the value of the request are questions to be decided with the deacons.

As for me, I have made a decision. In fact, my decision to support gay unions was made months, even years ago. The blessing of same-gender covenants is the church's overdue gift to gays and lesbians who seek support for loving, committed relationships. And their commitment will be a gift to the church. I've held that conviction for some time. At its core this decision is remarkably simple. A legitimate request for pastoral care has come to me. I am their pastor.

OCTOBER 18, 1991

I have been working on my statement of support to Eric and Ron's request. It is in the form of steps (or stepping stones) I have taken to arrive at this place of conviction. I think the deacons have the right to know what is behind my recommendation. And I hope it will help them clarify their own.

OCTOBER 21, 1991

I am experiencing a reality check. I'm in Richmond to join some brainstorming about the new Baptist seminary. I shared with former Pullen members Bob and Margaret last night the "stepping stones" narrative of my journey toward support of Eric and Ron's request. Today over coffee I did the same with Russ, another teacher and former Pullenite. All three seem shocked. They are vaguely supportive, but underneath I can feel their alarm. On the drive home I made sense of their surprise. While they are close friends over many years, they have not shared my recent history with gays and lesbians. I'm guessing that they have little or no history with this mostly invisible minority. Twelve years ago, if I had been presented this document by a friend, I would have been shocked out of my mind.

OCTOBER 25, 1991

Marv is a retired seasoned journalist, an acquaintance close enough for me to call. "I need some consultation," I tell him over the phone. "I'm dealing with a potentially explosive decision that has media implications. Would you talk with me?" "I'll stop by this afternoon," is his rapid reply.

At the beginning of our conversation, I acknowledge the possible conflict of interest. He is still working part time for a small newspaper in the area. "After I tell you my question, along with the background, if you choose not to comment, I will understand."

He nods, so I continue. I summarize the events that led to my support of Eric and Ron's request. "If this goes before the congregation eventually, what do you think the media response will be? Any advice?"

He makes no prediction. "It depends," he says. "If this creates a stir of interest within the community, then the media will consider it newsworthy. But, if there is little reaction, then expect little attention from the media."

He offers one strong word of advice: "If reporters call and want an interview, don't try to dodge. Dodging will only egg them on. Don't hide. Invite reporters in and give your perspective. Be prepared with what you want to say. And don't assume that anything is 'off the record.' Whatever you say is useable."

I can't tell if I have placed Marv in an awkward position. He keeps the visit short and to the point.

OCTOBER 31, 1991

At my request, Pat Long came by the office tonight. She is surprised to learn that I am almost at the point of asking the deacons to consider a same-gender ceremony. Seeking her advice earlier would have been inappropriate. She is a deacon now, and I haven't even made contact with the chair, Jim. Yet, I want her to read my statement that traces my step-by-step journey. She is a wordsmith and knows my story. I need her feedback, both on content and wording.

She likes the use of stepping stones as a metaphor, with each stone representing a step toward welcoming gays that includes the ritual of same-gender covenants. The statement provides a progression for the reader to follow.

It is not the statement that concerns Pat. She wonders about timing. It's a huge leap from the Forum discussions that involved a few members to a same-gender ceremony that might involve the entire congregation. Are the deacons and the congregation ready for such a leap? Has there been sufficient groundwork?

Again, I take refuge in the counsel of the deacons. They will decide whether or not to proceed. Conceivably, they may determine that more time and education are required. Then I would help Eric and Ron find another minister to perform a more private ceremony.

I am ready to proceed. I set up a time with Jim for tomorrow at 4:00.

NOVEMBER 1, 1991

Jim slowly reads my "stepping stones" statement in my office. Then he lays it aside, "I'm surprised and I'm not." He does not know either Eric or Ron, but he knows my thinking and has certainly observed the growing number and acceptance of gays within the congregation.

"This is my point of view, not what I expect others to believe," I remind him. "It is my best thinking on the matter." "I understand that," Jim responds quickly, "but there are years of study plus personal experience behind your convictions. How in the world are we going to bring into this conversation people who have never thought about homosexuality?"

We weigh the pros and cons of bringing the request to the deacons in their next meeting on Sunday night. "We have two deacon officers, let's check with them," he suggests.

During supper he calls me to say that he has arranged a breakfast meeting with Vic and Neil for tomorrow morning.

NOVEMBER 2, 1991

I join Jim, Neil, and Vic for breakfast this morning at the Brownstone Hotel. Like Jim, Neil and Vic are not totally surprised. Immediately they feel the weight of their responsibilities. They are the elected officers of the deacons, and in a larger sense, leaders of the congregation. They are thinking with the church in mind.

No one around the table thinks we should dodge it. All see the request as reasonable and an appropriate deacon matter to consider. There are questions about Eric and Ron, especially about their motivation. They then read the copy of my "stepping stones" statement that stimulates still more questions and comments. They want to proceed with presenting this request to the deacons on Sunday evening. "No sense in waiting," Vic says.

We agree that in tomorrow night's meeting, I will introduce the request as part of my Pastoral Report. At that time I will give the background of my meetings with Eric and Ron, then suggest that they read my "stepping stones" statement without comment on its content. Jim will say in advance that there will be no discussion on the request in that meeting. He will invite only questions of clarification. A separate meeting will be scheduled for deliberation.

I left the breakfast meeting, as perhaps they did, fully aware that we are about to enter another stage. The circle expands—from Eric, Ron and me, to the three of them, and tomorrow night to the deacons.

NOVEMBER 3, 1991

The gathering of deacons tonight seems routine. About twenty sit around tables in the "Seekers" class. As I scan the group, knowing the significance of the meeting, I appreciate the good mix of seasoned deacons alongside of newer deacons.

The update on our finances includes the usual wistful November hope for a strong finish in December. Progress on the search for a minister of education is reported. Finally we come to the last agenda item, my pastoral report.

I follow the plan worked out yesterday with Jim, Vic, and Neil. In my introduction to Eric and Ron's request, I urge the deacons to take the time needed for full discussion before any action is taken. "This decision is not mine to make," I remind them. "Only the congregation can authorize this extension of our ministry. We are discussing an additional ritual that would affirm gay covenant relationships."

"I want you to have my thoughts about this request," I continue. Then I distribute the description of the steps that led me to a position of support. As they are reading in silence, I think about the threshold we are crossing. The burden of this request, heavy on me for two months, is shifting to their shoulders.

Jim, after reminding them that no action will be taken at this meeting, asks them what information would help them in their consideration. A cluster of questions are asked about a "blessing" ritual. What does it look like? Are there historical precedents? Is it legal? How would it differ from a wedding ceremony? Also, the discussion includes its ramifications upon the church, our relationships with other Baptists, Eric and Ron and me.

The need for time is paramount. So much to understand in such a short time. A special called meeting is set for November 17. Jim asks that the meeting's information and discussion be treated as confidential.

The closing prayer, usually perfunctory, is laced with urgency tonight. Our yearning for guidance, our need for Presence is felt in the simple, carefully chosen words of petition by Leon.

NOVEMBER 17, 1991

Tonight the deacons continue their discussion of Eric and Ron's request. They engage the discussion with a level of honesty that I have seldom seen in church leaders. Having written my point of view, I am free to be pastoral, encouraging full participation. In truth, they don't need my encouragement. I say very little, only responding to an occasional request for information.

Jim, at the beginning, asks each person to share his or her thoughts about the request. It is evident that during the past two weeks there had been much study, prayerful reflection, and some confidential consultation with trusted friends. As each deacon shares, the others of us are asked to listen, not debate at this point. The deacons express very different positions: some in favor, others opposed, but most undecided. They want more time and information.

Pat Long has collected into notebooks some written resources for each deacon, mostly articles or excerpts about homosexuality from sermons and books. I'm thinking, these leaders look like students cramming for a final exam.

The deacons consider the impact of this request on people. Who would be hurt or helped by this ritual? The concern for the congregation is primary. Whatever decision is made, the church will be affected. Ripples of good and ill from their responses are inevitable.

Some look beyond Pullen. How will this request and the ultimate outcome affect our relationships in the Raleigh community, among Baptists and the larger church?

The most striking feature of tonight's discussion is Pat Long's role. Her position is unique, a respected deacon who is lesbian. Over a year ago, she acknowledged her orientation to the deacons. Last spring she was elected a deacon. Tonight she ventures another risk, speaking of a loving relationship with another well-respected woman in the congregation. This intimate friend died shortly before I came to Pullen in 1983. "It was the loneliness in my grief that I want you to understand," she says. "No one knew that we were more than friends. No one knew the size of the hole in my life where she had been. This is what living with secrets does to people. Most gays and lesbians must keep secret their sexual orientation but they do so with great cost and loss. If we are to be church to each other, our deepest joys and sorrows must be shared in community, not lived through alone."

As a deacon, Pat's testimony keeps our deliberations in the room. Without her presence, the focus would have been on a request from a member who is not personally known by most of the deacons. The interaction may have had an "out there" feel to it. With Pat in the circle, we know we are talking about our relationships—with Eric and Ron, for sure, but also with each other.

The meeting concludes with no agreement on recommendations. The deacons are taking their time. The next scheduled meeting is the first Sunday in December. Jim, once again, calls for confidentiality until a decision is made. Then he asks each one to give his or her response to the evening.

November 18, 1991

In reflecting on last night's discussion among the deacons, I am struck by the influence of Pullen's tradition. A few deacons identified the likely loss of members and finances if they take Eric and Ron's request to the congregation. Each time, in response, a reference was made to our history.

Elaine reminded us, "This wouldn't be the first time. We lost members over opening our membership to blacks. Then there were the years when Bill Finlator was speaking out against Vietnam. We lost members then, and money too. The church made it through. We can again if necessary."

In the past, Pullen's tradition has functioned like a sturdy keel, keeping our church upright in turbulent water. I felt its strength particularly last night. More than once it was identified as a steadying force beneath us.

I detect a slight shift in the deacon discussions. At first, the concerns are more immediate and institutionally directed, attention on the congregation, Ron and Eric, and understanding a same-gender ceremony. Now occasionally, theological questions and long-range thinking appear. How does Jesus relate to this request? How does this fit with our mission? Where is God in this?

The process is impressive. Listening is occurring. Astute questions are being raised. Opinions are being formed. The deacons are working very hard with a daunting responsibility.

NOVEMBER 28, 1991

In the last meeting, while no recommendations were made, an informal consensus emerged. The deacons agree that the approval of this ritual must involve the entire congregation.

Anticipating that action, Jim appointed a committee of five deacons to suggest ways the issue could be taken to the congregation. The committee met a week ago to prepare a plan.

This will be their recommendation: A letter will go to each church member that includes the recommendations from the deacons plus my "stepping stones" statement. Small meetings for members will be offered at various times and places where dialogue can occur within a climate of safety. Later, after the small groups, the committee envisions a town meeting, an "open mike" opportunity to gauge the will of the congregation without the pressure to vote. At the congregation meeting to follow, the congregation would decide whether they are ready to vote.

The deacons want to duplicate their experience with the congregation as much as possible. Their discussions have been respectful of each other's questions and different points of view. They want the same for the members.

DECEMBER 1, 1991

Once again Jim opens the meeting by asking each deacon to express his or her questions, thoughts, and feelings about the request. In this and other ways, Jim has kept each deacon engaged and valued. Then for over three hours, the deacons struggle, first to formulate the recommendations, then to refine the wording.

Tonight it became clear that the request is not primarily about Eric and Ron or about my right to perform such a service. Correctly, they focus on whether the blessing of same-gender unions would become a part of our ministry offered to members. By a vote of fourteen to five, they said it should.

There were moments when the deacons considered taking the request directly to the congregation without their recommendations. But they concluded that the congregation deserves the benefit of their best thinking, including those in opposition. They need to take a stand before asking the congregation to do so.

They will wait until January before taking these recommendations to the congregation. With all that is Advent and Christmas, trying to discuss these recommendations during December would sabotage the process and likely the season's celebrations as well.

The process committee, appointed by Jim, reports their plan for congregational discussion and eventual action on the same-gender ceremony. It is accepted with little comment and great appreciation. There's no energy for further work.

The deacons leave the meeting with the awareness that their most difficult work lies before them. As one comments, "If this has been tough for us to decide, how much harder will it be for the church."

DECEMBER 2, 1991

Jim has modeled for the other deacons their role during this next stage of congregational discussion. Deacons will be facilitators of the small discussion groups, fostering a safe climate and encouraging honest expressions of questions and convictions. They are not defenders or advocates of their recommendations. They are shepherds of an open process in search of faithful decisions.

These leaders have stepped up and assumed the responsibility to oversee this process. I marvel at their commitment.

DECEMBER 9, 1991

I relish being pastor during Advent. I love the traditions at this time of year—the call to waiting, the grace in gifts given and received, Jesus as centerpiece, and the backward glance before entering a fresh, new year. With both joys and sorrows accentuated during the holidays, pastoral care becomes a particular privilege.

And these weeks of Advent/Christmas offer some blessed relief. The topic, the church and homosexuality, has been our preoccupation, almost four months for me, five weeks for the deacons. May the season allow a deep, deep breath before the next wave of leadership hits us.

DECEMBER 30, 1991

Jim has been working on his letter to the congregation. It's scheduled for mailing on January 8. Along with the deacons' recommendations and my position statement of "stepping stones," the letter includes the proposed process for congregational dialogue. Jim wants the cover letter to reflect the tone and content of the deacons' discussions, including the major questions and differences.

JANUARY 2, 1992

Jim and I went to "school" tonight. We asked Edith Johnson to coach us in our relating to the media. Edith has experience with news reporting, both working with and for the media.

She reiterates what my journalist friend Marv counseled. Don't dodge the reporter's initiative, be succinct, know what you want to communicate and stick to it, and assume that everything you say is "on the record." Most helpful is the role-playing: Edith assuming the role of reporter; Jim and I are the interviewed.

We may be gearing up for a challenge that never comes. Given the volatility of the issue, we expect some attention.

JANUARY 6, 1992

I don't want my predecessor, Bill Finlator, to be surprised by the mail-out on Wednesday, so I invited him to lunch. We meet at Ballentine's, our favorite visiting place over the years. He doesn't expect any particular agenda today beyond our usual banter. Our common experience as pastors of

Pullen makes for great stories, lots of laughter, and unwavering support. He understands. He's been there.

I explain my reasons for lunch together. One, I want to alert him to the packet from the deacons to be mailed on Wednesday. And second, assuming that some Pullen members will call him, I hope that he will encourage them to participate in the process of discussions planned by the deacons. I want to, but hold back from asking him to favor the deacon recommendations.

Then, with some background explanation, I give him time to read the letter from Jim, my "stepping stones" statement, and the deacon recommendations. He takes his time reading, a very long time it seems to me. I have never discussed with Bill his views on homosexuality, or, even mine. So I don't assume agreement. We have talked about many other social issues, but not this one.

Finally he finishes. His eyes meet mine along with that impish grin of his. "Mahan, I would have dodged it. I wouldn't have picked this one up."

"I don't buy that, Bill. You wouldn't have dodged it," I respond without hesitation. "You never dodged a major justice concern in your time. On your 'plate' were the civil rights movement, Vietnam, and any other threat to civil liberties and human rights. The inclusion of gay Christians happens to fall on my 'plate.'" He smiles. I think he liked my response.

With no hint of reservation, he assures me of his support. When members call him, he will encourage them to join the process of discussion planned by the deacons.

Bill has some questions and comments. He wants to know more about the same-gender ceremony. He admits not being clear in his own thinking. "I've got some work to do."

Then he puts the fear of God in me. "Are you prepared, Mahan, to handle the fury that this will generate?" Bill knows something I don't. I sense it immediately. His words carry a frightening realism born of much experience with public controversy. A shiver goes down my spine. How would I know if I am prepared?

"I don't know if I am prepared. I do know my mind and heart. This conviction has been building in me for many years. But prepared? How can you ever know if you are ready for something like this?"

"You can't really," he admits. "But this is bold, I think prophetic. You'll get some heat."

JANUARY 7, 1992

I've been thinking today about my lunch with Bill and my entry in the journal last night. There's more to write.

Bill wants me to feel his support. And I do. But it is the deacons who are prophetic. And the deacons, in turn, are challenging the congregation to be as well.

Within the larger church today, there are clergy standing up for gay inclusion. There are voices from pulpits that speak of justice for homosexual persons. Some pastors support, as well, the value of same-gender ceremonies. My personal witness is not that unusual. What's unusual is for a congregation to dialogue and finally decide whether or not to offer a ritual of blessing upon same-gender covenants. That is indeed newsworthy. The discussion itself will be prophetic. An affirming decision will only make it more so.

Tomorrow the deacon letter goes out.

CHAPTER 7

Backing into a Whirlwind
January 9–February 1, 1992

JANUARY 9, 1992

YESTERDAY AFTERNOON JIM'S COVER LETTER and deacon packet were mailed. The deacons' recommendations will reach every member by tomorrow or Saturday.

I don't know how, but by this afternoon, the word is out. It raced through some incredible, invisible grapevine until someone alerted the *Raleigh News & Observer*. By 3:00 this afternoon, reporter Ayres Wilson was already on the phone asking for an interview.

I try to bargain with him: "Will you allow our congregation to have some time with our internal discussion about this request before it becomes so public? If you will wait, I promise your paper the full story." I can hear him laughing at my naïveté all the way to his supervisor. Of course, they want to break the story. Within moments the reporter calls back saying that a story will be written and published in tomorrow's paper. He hopes I will cooperate.

I imagine Marv over my left shoulder whispering: "Remember, don't be evasive. That makes reporters all the more eager." So, I invite him to my office. "I'll be right over," he tells me. We set a time for 4:30. And to think, a few weeks ago I was wondering if this story would be newsworthy.

The reporter was prompt, knocking on my office door precisely at 4:30. I open the door and face Ayres Wilson for the first time. My heart sinks. He looks so young! And this young, likely inexperienced reporter will have the first public word about Ron and Eric's request. Probably his article will reach the congregation before Jim's interpretative cover letter with the deacon packet.

My heart sinks further as the interview begins. Ayres is not only young, but he knows nothing about Baptist congregational polity and little about the subject of homosexuality. Remembering Edith's counsel, I take a deep breath and attempt to stay focused on what I regard as essential.

The interview with Ayres Wilson is cordial. I sense from him no "axe to grind" or no predisposed position to defend. To his credit, he works hard to understand. But my fear of his inexperience, so profound at the beginning, is never allayed. He, perhaps more than any other one person, will frame the issue beyond our congregation and probably within our church as well.

The curtain is up on the next act in this drama. In the previous acts I have felt some measure of control. If not a script to guide, we at least have followed an outline of sequential events. The conversations have been contained, first, with Eric and Ron, next with a few trusted friends, then finally within the deacons. The boundaries were clear. But now, Ayres's article and the deacon package to the congregation throw the conversation wide open. Any illusion of control is shattered.

JANUARY 10, 1992

I am relieved. Ayres Wilson's article, "Church asked to bless gay union," in the *Raleigh News & Observer* this morning is more accurate and positive than the article I had written in my anxious imagination.

Ayres honored my request to focus on the congregation, not on Ron and Eric or my role. "We believe in the wisdom of the congregation. It is our tradition to address contemporary concerns and injustices," he quotes me saying.

The quote from Neil Jackson is perfect. He is asked by Wilson if this will be a watershed for Pullen. Neil responds: "I don't know that this is a watershed—it comes naturally to Pullen [to deal with controversial issues]." A calm, reassuring response.

Wilson also noted the sense of struggle before us. From the deacons' letter, he lifts the words: "Our [deacons'] struggle has been difficult, sometimes painful. In the process we have experienced an exhilarating bond of respect and compassion, though differences remain."

I am reading the article through the eyes of many Pullen members who are facing a three-layered surprise—the request for a gay union, the deacons' recommendations, and immediate public attention. Through it all I hope they can see, not a decision made, but a decision *to be made* with "respect and compassion, though differences remain." I must say, this first public word is fair and factual.

JANUARY 11, 1992

Ayres Wilson's article in the *News & Observer* is picked up by the Associated Press. Today the *Durham Herald-Sun* carries an article with many of the same details and quotes. It begins: "Hard social issues are nothing new to Raleigh's Pullen Memorial Baptist Church." The *Greensboro News and Record* is the first paper to print the emphasis on covenant. The article reports my description of the church as a place for "the nurture of faithful covenants and the healing of broken covenants."

I expect this sudden publicity to be a flash in the pan. Then we can settle into the weeks of soul searching before us.

JANUARY 13, 1992

Our church secretary, Alice, more than any of us on the staff, is under fire, inundated with telephone calls. She is in the hot seat, trying to keep her cool, maintaining a pleasant voice, taking information, and assuring returned calls as soon as possible. Her calm tone can sometimes, but not always, ratchet down a notch or two the anxiety of the caller.

There is the full range of reactions from beyond Pullen. "Good for you. You have my prayers" to "How could you consider such a thing? Don't you know the scriptures condemn homosexuality?"

My RRNGLE friends are among the first to call. Jim Lewis wants to know what support he could offer. "I don't have time to talk," I tell him. "But how about calling me every few days for a couple of weeks and leave word with Alice that I am not crazy." This is crazy-making stuff.

Just as I feared, most members received the first word about the request from the newspaper or TV. The media are the first framers of the Pullen conversation. I wish that could have been otherwise. The deacons' packet invites response; the news reporting invites reaction. The deacons' letter offers a structure for members to respond in small communities. With the media, there is no structure for response. The deacons' packet is to the church family; the news goes out to the world.

The media includes television. WRAL camera men and interviewers were waiting for me in my office yesterday after worship. They were professional and considerate. But this afternoon the folks from Channel 11 barge in. No appointment. No courtesy. When I decline his request, the interviewer answered: "Well, a report will be on the news tonight regardless. You might as well have your say."

JANUARY 14, 1992

Now the letters are coming in. Is this not insane? All this reaction to a question—Will a church affirm the loving commitment of two gay men with a ritual?

"We have backed into a whirlwind," I said to the staff this morning. We were looking in one direction, attending to our internal request, when, all of a sudden, we feel the swirl of violent winds all around us. I expected a public breeze, even a gust, for a few days. I didn't expect a hurricane. We are into our seventh day with no letup in sight. No flash in the pan.

This image of a hurricane came to me yesterday when I am on the phone with Mickey, a gay man and Baptist from Fort Worth, with a call waiting from a reporter in Louisville, while someone else is knocking at the door. And looking out my window, I see the cameraman from WRAL getting out of his truck. Indeed, we have backed into a whirlwind!

And from an editorial in the Georgia Baptist state paper, I read that we are "throwing down the gauntlet" to Southern Baptists. That's a hoot! We are dealing with a member's admittedly controversial request. But taking on a denomination?

My retired journalistic friend Marv and I meet over coffee, once again "confidential and off the record." First thing, I tell him how useful his advice has been, including "never trust speaking 'off the record.'" He smiles at the inconsistency.

Marv seems slightly defensive. He hadn't anticipated such media interest. His surprise makes mine seem a little less naïve. He notes the number of "Letters to the Editor" beginning to appear. I had already mentioned the fifty-plus phone calls since last Friday.

He offers a word of advice. He questions my reference to "homophobia" in the first article where Ayres Wilson quotes me saying, "I'm very realistic about the depth of homophobia in our culture and in all of us." He doesn't challenge the truth of the statement. He challenges the implication that all those who oppose gay unions are homophobic.

He is right. As soon as he points this out, I see its truth. It is like accusing all opponents of Affirmative Action of being racist. Similarly, a person who opposes the same-gender ceremony is not necessarily motivated by the fear of homosexuality. If I want honest dialogue with thoughtful, faithful people, I must not accuse them of being homophobic. Marv is absolutely right.

JANUARY 15, 1992

While interest continues to surge beyond Pullen, the deacons are helping us stay focused. We are offering small group discussions these weeks at all times of the day. Some are in members' homes, some at the church. Written resources are available in the library. The deacons are doing all they can to provide a safe, supportive climate for discernment in the midst of this whirlwind. It's tough, attempting a family conversation in the public square.

Letters are pouring in, both here at the church and in the Letters to the Editor section of the *Raleigh N & O.* The negative message is consistent: we urge you, Pullen, to honor the biblical mandate against homosexuality and vote against the recommendation of the deacons. They regard any affirmation of homosexual behavior as sinful. To bless a marriage-like ceremony is unthinkable.

An example is a letter from a nearby pastor: "You have departed from that which is Christian, which is Biblical, and which is Southern Baptist . . . . God saves us from our sin, not in our sin! Therefore, blessings from God or His Church upon a lifestyle of deliberate and continuing sin are out of order at the very least . . . the privilege of autonomy is being viewed by the world as well as many Christians as simply a license to sin."

There are an equal number of supportive letters. My RRNGLE friends are writing to the *Raleigh N & O.*

I particularly appreciate Sally Zumbach's speaking up for the parents: "We parents have learned to be free from any burden of guilt for our children's sexual orientation. We recognize their expression of love as natural for them and moral. We love and affirm our children with pride and are committed to their entitlement to full civil and human rights."

A few letters, like this personal note from a young pastor, affirm the struggle: "I appreciate the approach of the congregation in having a rational discussion of this matter. . . . Although I am uncertain myself as to what to make of homosexuality, I am encouraged to know that other Christians are struggling honestly to find a loving response."

JANUARY 16, 1992

What a pleasant surprise this morning! I open the *Raleigh N & O* to see Jim Jenkins' supportive column on the editorial page. His title: "At Pullen, still more room in the envelope." It could not have come at a better time.

Jim, who grew up at Pullen, lifted up our tradition of dealing with difficult issues. He kindly placed me in the middle of that tradition. He framed my advocacy for a gay union as consistent with the spirit of former pastors, E. McNeil Poteat and W. W. Finlator. Jim adds, "This is not an act of whimsy, ego, or sensationalism. For any pastor of Pullen, asking tough questions is part of the job description."

Jim put words to my hope: "Through it all, he has followed his own conscience, inviting those who agree to join him, but understanding that those who do not agree can be part of the Pullen family, too."

Jim framed our controversy within the larger context of Pullen history. He reminds his readers, including I hope our members, that this current consideration is consistent with our heritage.

JANUARY 17, 1992

Charles McMillan, Director of Missions of our Raleigh Baptist Association, calls on behalf of Silas Foster, the chair of the Association's Mutual Care Commission. Silas wants the three of us to meet. In our conversation Charles said that they have received numerous calls about Pullen. I assume each call is an expression of alarm and dismay.

Silas, Charles, and I met this afternoon. Silas brings his Bible; I have mine. He begins with, "Mahan, you should resign as a member of the Mutual Care Commission. You have lost your credibility."

After our exhausting dialogue of two hours, I go back to his request that I resign. "I can resign, Silas, but let's consider an option. Since the Mutual Care Commission has as its purpose to help congregations deal constructively with conflict, why don't we model this option? I much prefer it to resigning."

Surprisingly, Silas agrees. We decide to go to other members of the Commission with this proposal: that the Mutual Care Commission sponsor an open, public discussion about Pullen's request for a gay union ceremony. He promises to call a meeting of the Commission.

I respect Silas. I expected passionate conviction, but not openness.

JANUARY 19, 1992

We were gathering in the library at 6:00 for our monthly meeting of the lay pastoral care team. I overhear this conversation between two of Pullen's finest. It's a microcosm of Pullen responses to the request from Ron and Eric.

Allison and Edna are good friends, long-time members of Pullen, and like all of us have the gay ceremony on their minds. Allison exclaims, "Edna, isn't this an exciting time! Why, I have never even thought about homosexuality, but now I am learning so much, both from the reading and the groups. Don't you feel this way?"

Edna's response is chilling. "No. I do not! Don't even talk to me about it. I resent having to deal with a question I have never raised, nor intend to consider."

A few reactions don't fit this continuum between Allison and Edna. For some the request is a non-issue. "What's the big deal? I've had gay friends for years." Another set of members protest: "Mahan, I don't have time or energy to give to this. It's crazy these days at work. I don't need for it to be crazy at church as well."

JANUARY 20, 1992

A letter of opposition came across my desk today. It is the first communiqué from one member to other members that I have seen.

In his well-crafted letter, John takes a strong stand against a "pseudo-marriage ceremony of like gender participants as a church function." He regards such a ceremony to be not only detrimental to the church, but to larger society as well.

His central concern is the family. By endorsing same-gender unions we would "nullify support for the normal family relationships . . . ." He concludes: "To cloud the past, and dim the future of our church by this act is unbelievable and incomprehensible."

For John, a gay ceremony in our sanctuary conducted like a wedding ceremony would affirm the formation of a different form of family. He is correct about that. He rightly names this discussion as a challenge to our familiar ways of defining family. This point helps me understand the outrage. What is more basic than the family?

JANUARY 21, 1992

Thank God for other work to do.

Last Wednesday night I led a discussion on Martin Luther King, Jr. Other Wednesday night offerings included the study of Ezekiel and a seminar on the evoking of personal, spiritual gifts. A new cycle of Foyer groups [small getting-acquainted groups meeting in homes] begin again this month, and this is our month to help with the overflow shelter for the homeless. A missions fair is planned for the twenty-ninth to highlight ten local, national, and international mission projects. Then, of course, there are the grounding weekly gatherings for corporate worship plus the steady calls for pastoral care.

JANUARY 22, 1992

The content of Joy's letter has stayed with me. She verbalizes the fear among us—the question of timing. For her, this is the challenge: "I want straight people to struggle, examine their fears, ask questions, receive answers, feel uncomfortable, and grow. All gay people who aren't severely depressed have gone through that process. I want gays to learn patience with the struggle, to accept genuine confusion and fear, to feel free to answer questions, and to offer support without judging. I think the Deacons have a good plan. My main worry is that it took me years to accept myself and we expect the congregation to do it in a month!"

Should the leaders, including me of course, have gone slower, putting in place a longer educational process? Or, does it take a specific request like Eric and Ron's to mobilize a serious consideration of a controversial issue?

JANUARY 23, 1992

There are ramifications from these discussions that none of us anticipated. For instance, Laura fears being "outed" by this discussion. Someone might suspect that she is homosexual. Beyond a few friends, she is not ready to be known as a lesbian. "I feel guilty for withdrawing for a time," she tells me over the phone today.

Then I heard about Susan. Her former husband, without notice, announced that he was gay and in love with another man. She was left with two preteen boys. Understandably, she sees the congregational discussion through the lens of her devastating experience. She too is pulling back.

I think of families protecting the secret of a gay son or daughter. And there must be marriages in our midst where one is a "closeted" homosexual. How can any of these members participate in this open dialogue? How are they handling this very public conversation? It is like an iceberg, and we see only the tip. Most reactions remain hidden, invisible beneath the surface.

Wayne Oates, my major professor in doctoral studies, calls today. He had read in the Louisville paper about the fury generated from the request. He asks two questions: "How are you doing? How is the church doing?" He shows no interest in discussing the "why" of my actions. That conversation will come later. Today his call is pastoral.

JANUARY 24, 1992

Gene Puckett, editor of our state Biblical Recorder (Southern Baptist), stated his view in this week's editorial. First, he affirmed our autonomy as a congregation. Decisions about ministry are congregational.

Then he concludes: "[Pullen has] gone one step too far in their considerations. But unless one is a member of the congregation, opinions are all we can have and the congregation should not be intimidated by external forces in making their final decision, whether it be right or wrong. Local Baptist churches have the right to be wrong and in this case Pullen . . . [is] wrong, dead wrong."

Are we dead wrong for having the discussion?

In this week's Pullenews Jim reflects to the congregation the spirit and content of the first week of small-group meetings. In the four meetings he attended Jim notes, "We have listened to each other and learned from each other even though, in some cases, our views differ. It is important that we can disagree yet continue to love one another."

He gives sample comments of the "diversity and depth of the discussion" which included: "Will this label Pullen a gay church?" . . . "I wish we did not have the newspapers involved" . . . "If being gay is genetically transmitted then I have no problem. If it is a learned experience, I want to protect my son" . . . "Pullen is the first church in 30 years where I have felt free to worship God" . . . "Will this create a problem for Pullen members in their place of employment?" . . . "Sometimes it is painful to ask what God would have us do."

He ends with a call to prayer: "I urge your prayers as we continue to discern the will of God and to be faithful to our calling in Christ."

JANUARY 25, 1992

Last night I met with our youth at the request of their leaders. It was damage control, an attempt to recover from leaving the youth out of our planning.

Some of them are embarrassed and confused by the public attention to Pullen in the community. "Oh, you go to that faggot church," a few have heard at school. But, given the chance, most have opinions about gays, I discover. As far as I know, there are no gay persons in the youth group, but over half of our youth know gays that are "out" at school. The inhibition to talk, often felt by adults, is absent among them.

I regret this oversight. We have failed to offer biblical and theological grounding to their "locker room" knowledge. They have heard no stories from our mature gay members, like Pat. Furthermore, as our discussion tonight reveals, a few of the youth feel caught between parents who differ in their responses to the request from Ron and Eric.

For adolescents who generally don't want to stick out in the crowd, being identified with Pullen has done just that. This opportunity for support and education is not totally lost, but almost.

The public fascination with Pullen's open discussion of a same-sex union persists. There is no let up. It's as if Pullen has told a family secret. We are acknowledging openly that gays and lesbians are in our midst. Have we named a truth that others have conspired to avoid?

Telling the secret changes everything. Most families don't want to know, and most churches don't want to know. "Don't ask, don't tell" is not just a military policy. The military services borrow what has been operative in both families and churches for centuries. Have we at Pullen, unknowingly, come along with a mirror in our hands, saying, "Look, there are gay Christians in our midst who have gifts to bring, needs to share and service to offer"?

We are not the only church shining the spotlight on what has been kept in darkness. The Unitarian Universalist Fellowship and the United Church of Christ congregation in our area have been "out front," ahead of us for years. Fundamentalist churches turn the light on homosexuality in a condemning way. But most mainline churches choose not to turn on the light at all. When I think of the reaction to Jimmy Creech and now to us, the telling of a family secret provides some sense to these surprising reactions, both their volume and quantity.

JANUARY 28, 1992

I am hearing from Jim and the staff that the group meetings are not satisfactory for members who don't feel free to share their opinions with gays present in the groups.

The deacons struggled with this very question in their planning. One option considered: let some groups be "gay free"; let other groups have gays present. They rejected this option for fear it would foster a "we"-"them" kind of thinking. Besides, the deacons experienced Pat Long as a positive resource in their discussions. They hoped that other gays within the small groups would also enhance, not inhibit the dialogue.

Eric, Ron, and I decided not to attend these group meetings. We figure that our presence might limit the freedom of expression. Members know my position from the "stepping stones" paper. It is available for them to read. As for Eric and Ron, the deacons want the focus on the same-gender ceremony, not on them.

JANUARY 29, 1992

I failed to record yesterday an important piece of my conversation with Jim. While I was away for a few days, he and Pat Long were discussing the options before us. "What if," Jim was wondering, "we decide now to welcome gays and lesbians into full membership and pick up later the more controversial question about the same-gender ceremony?"

Jim reports Pat's response. "If we welcome gays into membership, we accept them as individuals. If we adopt the covenant ceremony, we affirm also their sexuality and its expression within a committed relationship. The first option accepts only a part of the person, leaving for later the implications of their sexuality."

The stage one, stage two approach, is a political solution we hope can be avoided.

Dissenting voices are more forthcoming now. One member states his dilemma: "How can dissenting voices be expressed without appearing uncaring or unchristian?" That's a challenge.

He begins his letter by acknowledging the need of the church to oppose the economic and vocational discrimination against homosexual persons. Yet he sees the blessing of a holy union as too extreme at this point in time. He itemizes the negative consequences: More and more homosexuals will be coming to Pullen; more ceremonies of such holy unions will be requested; many heterosexual couples—especially those with children—will feel uncomfortable in Pullen's congregation; the demographics of the church will change considerably; Pullen will tend to become a single issue church; focus on this issue, which reaches to the core of our subconscious, physiologic being, will interfere with worship; Pullen's credibility in the community will be diminished; Pullen's interaction with Martin Street Baptist Church (our partner African-American congregation) will be jeopardized; and Pullen's congregation will become more transient with limited stability provided by multigenerational families.

He adds: "Finally, one should not ignore the innate emotional reaction of most heterosexual persons when they come in close contact with homosexual lovers. . . . Can we not strive for better acceptance of homosexuals in our society without damaging Pullen Church through unrealistic expectations of its heterosexual members?"

A group of eight local Baptist pastors came to see me this afternoon. Alice had scheduled the appointment while I was away. Their concern, of course, is our open discussion on the request from Ron and Eric. They ask that our church step back from this public affirmation of sin.

I wonder why they came. Maybe they are obeying the Gospel of Matthew's directive in chapter 18—go to your brother, confront him of his sin, appeal for his confession, and seek reconciliation upon repentance. They are protective of our Baptist image in the community. Pullen, in their mind, is tarnishing that image. They are polite and honest, and, I think, curious. "How could a fellow Baptist pastor support such a request?" I'm an enigma to them.

I pique some interest when I tell them about Pat, Darrell, and Eric and Ron's desire for a blessing from God and their church family upon their covenant love. A couple of them tell stories about gays and lesbians who have been healed of their homosexual desires. Christ has changed them.

From these pastors I hear the familiar arguments for viewing all homosexual behavior as sinful. In turn I give my typical responses. We all seem to be following set scripts.

JANUARY 30, 1992

The Poteat Sunday Class—a group of mostly elderly members—sent to the deacons their "almost unanimous consensus": "The request comes to the church AS AN ORGANIZATION primarily as a political effort to further the agenda of homosexuals in this community. . . Individual members of the church could participate in ceremonies of this nature outside the church according to the dictates of their own conscience without seriously affecting the basic functions and the effectiveness of the church . . . . Therefore the class reacts very strongly against the request."

JANUARY 31, 1992

Ruth calls this morning while I am putting finishing touches to Sunday's sermon. She is an important figure to me and to Pullen, a community that she has loved for over thirty years.

Her words hit hard. "Mahan, this is going to split the church! Can't you do something?" she begins. "My friends tell me that they will leave if the church goes through with this request of the gay couple. Some may leave anyway. They are embarrassed, Mahan. They are tired of defending Pullen in social and work settings, especially since they don't think we should be having this discussion in the first place. And again this morning, I see another letter to the editor in the *Raleigh N&O.* I dread to pick up the paper. Mahan, Pullen is no longer the church we have enjoyed through the years."

"What do you see that I could do?"

"Well, you were the one to start us down this road. People respect you, Mahan. If you urged the church to back away from this decision, they would listen to you."

"I cannot do that, Ruth. For one thing, such an effort from me would undermine the deacons who designed and are leading the process before us. And honestly, Pullen's relationship with gay Christians is too important for me to shelve, even if it were possible."

"Well, you could go to the deacons. They know what's happening. They could stop this thing, even postpone the decision."

"This could still happen," I remind Ruth. "This Sunday afternoon the congregation will gather to assess the state of this process. It's a Town Meeting where opinions, questions, and feelings can be voiced. The purpose of this meeting is to take the pulse of the congregation. I hope you and your friends will come and express what you have shared with me."

I end the conversation with an effort to be upbeat. "Ruth, I hope that what unites us—our worship of God, our commitment to Christ, our long history of mutual friendships, our memories of shared joy and pain—will be strong enough to hold us together in our differences."

"That sounds nice," she says with unresolved frustration. "In this case, I don't think the center will hold." Her last words stun me.

I hang up the phone and begin to work through what has become a familiar regimen when anxiety attacks with full force. The questions line up like hurdles in a steeplechase: "What have I done to this century old congregation?" to "What can I do to fix this crisis?" to "Whose church is this anyway?" to "Why did I start down this path with Ron and Eric?" to "How can I stay centered?" to "How can I stay connected?" to "Can I trust the wisdom in this congregation?" and finally, to "Can I trust that God is at work for good in this?" It can take anywhere from days or hours or minutes to jump over these hurdles.

Later this afternoon, of all people, Mitch calls. What a pleasant surprise to hear from an early mentor.

Mitch's familiar voice immediately takes me back to our three years of working together in the early '60s. Mitch, now a priest in Atlanta, had read about the controversy in his local paper.

Mercifully, he doesn't ask me to rehearse the details. After some brief exchanges, he offers me a story.

Some years ago in Waco, I attended a retirement dinner for a feisty, outspoken Methodist minister. Someone commented, "Jim, you have been in the midst of many controversies during your ministry." Jim nodded in acknowledgement. "Well then," the man continued, "Tell us what most helped you in those times?"

"Well," Jim came back, "There is a verse I would repeat."

"Tell us! Tell us! What is the verse?" the man persisted.

"Well," Jim came back, "The verse I would pull out in tough times goes like this: 'The Lord is my shepherd . . . what the hell!'"

Soon he hung up and I was left to interpret. I hear two words in his story: God is our shepherd. Take comfort in this guiding, caring Presence. And second, hang loose. Don't care so much about controlling results. Do your best. Offer it up.

February 1, 1992

The weeks of small group meetings have ended. In the Town Meeting tomorrow we test the pulse of the congregation. Then at the congregational meeting on February 9, we will decide whether or not we are ready to vote.

I find this remarkable. During these past weeks, all these deliberations about the same-sex ceremony have been laid on top of on-going obligations. Members, as always, are busy with the daily rounds of bills to pay, families to feed, homework to finish, and schedules to meet. Meanwhile at church, the financial books on 1991 were closed. Committees met. The church school entered a new year. Wednesday night programs resumed. Our annual participation in Martin Luther King holiday events occurred. The request from Ron and Eric was inserted somewhere in their list of priorities. For most members, obligations have been set aside in order to engage this discussion. They have found a way to participate.

During these Sundays I have refrained from addressing the *content* of the deacon recommendations. The church has my written statement. In worship I have remained pastoral, praying for God's guidance and encouraging participation and confidence in our process of discernment. Tomorrow I want the sermon to offer a context for the Town Meeting scheduled in the afternoon.

I'm preaching on the lectionary text from Jeremiah 31. Jeremiah anticipates a new covenant, a new Torah to be written upon the heart. The Torah (the Law) for the Hebrew, as I explain in the first part of the sermon, offers clues to the mystery of God's intention. It is not a list of regulations to follow. Jeremiah understood that God's will cannot be externally codified into laws but finally must be discerned in the heart, which for the Hebrew is the place of inner thought and intuition.

Then I proceed to the New Testament passage where Jesus announces to his disciples that in his absence the "paraclete," his alongside spirit will lead them. My paraphrase of Jesus: "I'll not be around as a separate person to answer your questions and tell you what to do. My spirit, God's spirit will be with you and in you to guide you. Find me in your heart."

From that biblical base I turn to the decision before our congregation:

A male church member, Eric, has requested that the monogamous, committed union between himself and another male, Ron, receive the blessing of God, family and friends in this church. And we have responded: What would God have us do? We look for external examples of same-gender covenants in the Torah and find none. We look for external instructions from Jesus and find none. We are left on our own to search for guidance from the internal Law, the Torah of God written on our hearts. We are left to our search for the spirit of Jesus within us, alongside of us, between us.

Being Baptists, we do not leave the interpretation of God's will to popes or priests or pastors, and not to creeds or deacons or chance. On matters of faith and practice we seek to internalize both the Torah and the spirit of Jesus, asking together what would God as creator have us be, what would God as spirit have us become? Why *together?* Because within the faith community, past and present, is our best chance of discerning God's will for us in our day.

This has been a painful month for many of us. We know the pain of being at odds with persons we love and respect. We have heard family, friends, colleagues and strangers criticize our church for being irresponsible and morally wrong. Some of us experience the frustration of being pushed into dealing with a concern not of our choosing and one for which we didn't feel ready. There is among us the pain of being labeled homophobic if we oppose the recommendation from the deacons. The pain of not feeling heard or understood is also our experience. Then, there are sighs of anguish, as Paul says, "too deep for words."

There is fear among us as well: the fear that irreparable damage is being done to our church; the fear of obsession over one issue, to the neglect of other worthy concerns; the fear that evil power in threats, misinterpretations, rejection, deception and sabotage will overcome the power of honesty, respect, cooperation, listening, and mutual faith in God at work for good in everything with those called to God's purposes.

As part of our worship, we offer to God our pain and fear this morning. But let us bring before God our celebration, as well. I celebrate, and invite you to celebrate, being a part of a congregation that did not treat a fellow member as invisible nor his request as unimportant. I give thanks for our collective courage to confront a pastoral and prophetic concern that will be on the larger church's agenda for years to come. We can celebrate the struggles of faith, the learning, the listening, and the questions about God and church and covenants.

So, along with the pain and fear and gratitude, let us bring our faith as trust to this Table of Communion. Trust the wisdom of God written in our hearts. Trust the wisdom of God written in our heritage. Trust the promise of the Spirit, the "paraclete," the alongside presence of Christ among us.

Let us now, from the heart, approach this Table together. Let us pray for the miraculous to occur again—that the God embodied in Jesus grant us the privilege of being the body of Christ, the people of God in our day.

CHAPTER 8

The Eye of the Storm

February 2–29, 1992

FEBRUARY 2, 1992

ONLY THEOLOGICAL LANGUAGE WILL DO. For me, the Town Meeting this afternoon was a sacred moment. A sense of group spirit, esprit de corps. The Spirit seemed to stir among us like the wind. Members spoke with unusual clarity. Some, typically verbose, were concise and compelling. Others, often quiet, were bold in their differing perspectives. There was a rare quality of listening, seeking, and risking as members spoke from the heart.

Jim, once again, provided effective leadership. He set the stage with guidelines about confidentiality and procedures for the open-microphone sharing. He reminded the several hundred members packed tight in Finlator Hall that the purpose of the meeting is dialogue. Voting, debate, and parliamentary procedures will be next Sunday's agenda.

The first two members to speak oppose the blessing of a same-gender union. One addresses the threat of this possible decision both to church and family. He touches the fear common to all, the potential negative impact on our congregation. His second point is equally relevant: we are considering a redefinition of family. He expresses forceful objections to the deacon recommendations.

The other person is less persuasive, but no less passionate in his opposition. Both men are heard with respect. The meeting is off to a good start, I tell myself.

Others begin speaking for the gay union from very different perspectives. One couple, soon to be married, says that the privilege that belongs to them should be available to Eric and Ron. A few parents want a learning community for their children that includes friendships with both homosexuals and heterosexuals. Some gays speak at great risk, a few for the first time in public. One member suggests that the same-gender ceremony counters the stereotype of gays as always single and promiscuous. Another notes the suicide of a gay loved one.

There are occasional theological questions: What is God's will in all of this? How does this fit with our mission? Miriam, a wisdom figure among us, keeps before us the mandate: "What would Jesus do?"

It is the common desire to do the right thing that moves me so. The care for the church and its mission became the central passion. The stakes are high, felt by everyone. The best in us was being called forth to meet a challenge that we know is changing us in unknown ways.

I am not the only one who sensed the Spirit among us. At the monthly deacon's meeting tonight, Allen Preston calls the Town Meeting an "Upper Room" experience. James McBride adds, "It was like a revival."

FEBRUARY 3, 1992

Today I am living with the down side of yesterday's spirited town meeting. Members with longevity are concerned, members who have invested in Pullen's life for thirty, forty, even fifty years. The combined money and time they have given to Pullen far exceeds what the rest of us have contributed. They intuit a sea change. Whatever the outcome of Eric and Ron's request, Pullen will be different. I see it as well. This coming vote is as much about the nature of Pullen's mission as it is about a particular ritual. Even if the church decides to reject or postpone a decision on the ceremony, we are making a commitment to gay Christians in this process from which we will not withdraw. And gay members are making a commitment to Pullen from which they will not withdraw.

Some of these older members are facing a tough decision. They confront a question that they thought would never be before them, namely, can I stay at Pullen? These few (and I don't know how many) likely assume that someday they would be buried from this sanctuary led by a pastor who knows them. They have imagined Pullen friends bringing food and making visits when the threats of aging overtake them. In leaving they have so much to lose. I can only glimpse the trauma of entering a new, strange congregation at this time in their lives.

Then I think of Mary Jane. She also represents those with many years at Pullen. I see the sparkle in her eyes these days. She couldn't be more proud of her church. She's excited about the process, obviously enjoying its fruits of learning and new friendships.

As I told the deacons last night when they asked how I was doing, "I have never felt such pain and joy at the same time."

February 5, 1992

A member new to our congregation read a letter to the congregation during the Town Meeting last Sunday. He describes his first reaction:

Unlike many gay members of Pullen, I first learned that Mahan had been asked to bless a same-gender union when I received the letter from the Deacons. I confess that my first reaction was one of dismay. I have been comfortable. I wondered whether the inevitable controversy engendered by this issue would make it uncomfortable for me to be a Pullen member, and I resented the church's being forced to undergo this upheaval. I'm glad to say that I soon passed beyond that bit of selfishness, in part because I became convinced that our Deacons have very thoughtfully constructed a process for addressing this issue which can make it possible for sharply conflicting and highly-charged opinions to be exchanged in a non-confrontational way.

Lately I've asked myself whether my past ten months [with his partner] would have been easier had we been blessed . . . had we had the chance to stand up before you and God and affirm our commitment to each other. Of course, it is impossible to say. . . what is presented to Pullen at this moment in its history is an opportunity to affirm love and commitment, no matter what our feelings might be about homosexuality and sin. I hope—I pray— that this opportunity will not slip away . . . And whatever the outcome, I'll be here.

February 6, 1992

This week is slow moving. Another time of waiting. Looming over us all is the curiosity, if not fear, about this coming Sunday's outcome. Friends, including Janice and the children, have made the waiting tolerable.

About Janice. She, more than anyone else, has made bearable this extended period of stress. Being with her is grounding. She represents the commitments, memories, and joys that remain when the storm subsides. Yesterday she said, "It is like you are away fighting a war. I'm covering here, and I know you will come back when it is all over."

I have no lack of support, not only from family but also from a close circle of male friends. But Janice is in difficult spot, experiencing our stressful time, yet not being able to do much about it. I have things to do. She, on the other hand, stands by, knowing my fatigue, seeing me wince from the criticism, observing my joy over someone that she doesn't know. Her suffering, even the joy of convictions we shared, has a poignancy that few people see.

There are graceful exceptions along the way. One day last week Janice comes home to discover at the front door a box of chocolates with this attached note, "Janice, some sweets for the bitter time," signed, Mary Lib Finlator. One wife of a former Pullen pastor to the current one. Mary Lib understands completely.

February 7, 1992

Two weeks ago a policeman from the bomb squad came to Janice. In response to the uproar in the larger community over Pullen's process, the officer talked to her about precautions against threats to our lives. He told her of a few specific violent acts against families of gay rights advocates in North Carolina. "Suspect any package from some one or some place unfamiliar to you, especially if it comes from the Sanford area," he counseled.

Well, it happened. Today we received a package from a Parker Henderson in Sanford. Not recognizing the name, Janice called the police. Within minutes, two policemen appear. The package looks suspicious. Promptly they don their protective uniforms and carefully open the package. And what do they find? A tarnished bracelet!

It turns out that the bracelet was a gift from our son, Marshall. He had given it to Parker, his high school sweetheart over ten years ago. She is moving to California and came across the gift while packing. What timing!

February 8, 1992

Tomorrow afternoon will be the long anticipated congregational meeting. The time for deciding whether or not to vote has arrived.

In the morning, I am choosing to frame my sermon within our distant Anabaptist heritage. I will recall my experience of standing at the spot on Lake Zurich where Felix Manz, the Anabaptist martyr in the sixteenth century, was torturously drowned for his belief in adult baptism. I imagine his word to us:

Along comes Feliz Manz, and the other Anabaptists, saying, "It's not enough to be born into the church. It's not even enough to learn the catechism and creeds and repeat them by heart." "To be a Christian," they insist, "is to answer a call, a call not just to believe, but a call to behave in a certain way, a call to follow the way of Christ." Following Christ (Nachfolge Christi) was their hallmark.

Later in the sermon I speak to the situation before us.

As we all know this morning, a demanding responsibility has been laid before us as a congregation . . . We have an ethical decision to make with awesome consequences. . . . In Anabaptist fashion, each believer is a priest; each of us is challenged to discern our best reading of God's will. Each of us must decide what it means to follow Jesus with regard to this request. There is nowhere to hide. As if coming to our decision were not difficult enough, we are challenged to respect and listen to other members who differ from us and defend their right to do so. What a high demand we take upon ourselves—to speak the truth as we see it in love.

And there is another demanding dimension. We must declare our sense of God's intentions before the public eye. Like it or not, our struggle is a witness to the community. Many are watching to see if members of this congregation can love God and each other more than they love having their way . . . . Many are watching to see if we can offer to the divisive world an example of a reconciling community. We are on the witness stand.

Once again our Anabaptist heritage can help us. The Anabaptists could live with the tension of a highly demanding gospel because they have an equally high view of grace. Their understanding of the sacrificial cost of following Christ is matched by their sense of God's unmerited, unconditional love. They could venture much because they are forgiven much.

To be specific, we will gather this afternoon as "sinners saved by grace." That's the way Felix Manz might say it. This affirmation can help us as we feel the great responsibility of deciding our own sense of Christian conscience. We realize our point of view will be contaminated by self-interest. Our grasp of the gospel will be partial. The motive behind our vote will not be absolutely pure. We need the openness and humility that only undeserved forgiveness gives . . .

We've learned again this month, like our ancestors the Anabaptists, how wonderful and frightening the gospel can be. We've learned the cost of being church—the pain, the fear, the strain in relationships. And we have learned, as well, the joy of being church, sensing the courage and goodness and power in our relationships. . . We are learning to trust each other within the larger invitation to trust the promised Spirit in our midst . . .

Tomorrow I want the worship service, including the sermon, to place in context this historical moment.

February 9, 1992

The Poteat Class that had sent the letter of opposition to the deacons last week was in prayer this morning. Their Sunday School class is praying for our congregational meeting this afternoon. The conclusion of Mike Watts's prayer captures their angst:

> So Lord, we find ourselves on the horns of a dilemma. We want to do right, but we don't want to be unwise or too hasty in our actions. . . . And finally, Lord, whichever way the decision goes, may we continue to love and be loved by our brothers and sisters with whom we may differ. And grant us, Lord, the serenity to accept the things we cannot change, the courage to change what can and should be changed, and the wisdom to know the difference. Amen.

At 3:00 the sanctuary is full, over 300 members in the lower pews, probably forty active non-members in the balcony, and the media cameras and crew outside. No doubt this is the largest and maybe the most important congregational meeting in Pullen's history.

Whatever the actions taken today, this church will be changed. Everyone knows this truth on some level. The anxiety expresses itself in multiple ways. I see it in the nervous chattering among Diane, Margaret and Ann, close friends for many years. I see it in the stern, intense look on Russell's face, and Mary and Lee's also, as they wait for the meeting to begin. In silence most members file down the aisles and take their seats.

This mood is in stark contrast to the reverent anticipation that precedes the weekly worship service. This time there is no organ prelude. No lighted candles. No bulletin to read or finger. Only a tense stillness prevails. Unfortunately, this is not a sanctuary this afternoon.

Jim calls us to order, and order begins to come. He sets the tone with his statement of purpose and calming presence.

There are two surprises that soon surface. One, the deacons introduce their revised recommendations. The deacons met early this morning at the Brownstone, and, based on their learning from these weeks of group discussions, drafted a graduated set of motions. The first is a general affirmation of Pullen's ministry of reconciliation. The second is a more specific motion to welcome all persons into membership without regard to sexual orientation. The third motion is the affirmation of same-gender ceremonies, and the final motion proposes a task force to examine the biblical and theological foundations of a same-gender ritual of blessing. The deacons decided against one "yes" or "no" on the request. They offer options.

The other surprise is the motion to mail ballots to all members. At that point, some relax, feeling relief that a public showdown might be avoided. Others protest: "The members sufficiently motivated to attend this meeting should decide the outcome!" Still others counter: "This decision is too important to exclude any members." One member adds, "I know of six members who could not be here today. Shouldn't they be allowed to vote?" The motion to mail out the ballots passes by a sizeable majority. From that point the rest of the meeting focuses on the wording of the four recommendations from the deacons.

One amendment is particularly significant. It includes: "that no rituals of the church be denied to any member of Pullen on the basis of sexual orientation alone." If passed, the door to the ordination of gays and the inclusion of gay parents in the child dedication services is opened. The wording of that amendment passes with little discussion.

Most everyone who came to this meeting believed that, at last, a decision would be made. The time of closure on this emotionally charged request had come, so it seemed. But closure is postponed. This afternoon we add another month. Since Jim and I had little to report, the frustration of indecision included the media as well. A mailed-out ballot has little news appeal.

February 10, 1992

The ballots are mailed out today with the notice that they must be returned to the church by 5:00 PM on February 27.

In the last paragraph of the cover letter, Jim writes: "I appreciate our prayerful consideration of these motions . . . and I trust that the wisdom of the congregation, guided by the Holy Spirit, will lead us to a deeper experience of what it means to be church together."

FEBRUARY 11, 1992

This brief respite from the intensity of the gay union discussion is welcome. Once again, we are waiting.

Periods of waiting throughout these months, like little advents, have provided fertile interludes between the more public seasons. Early in the process, a month of waiting follows my initial sessions with Eric and Ron. Then the deacons wait during the December month of Advent before they present their recommendations to the congregation in January. During this past month, the small groups, study and worship provide an intentional waiting period of processing that preceded the voting scheduled for last Sunday.

Now, by choosing to mail the ballots, we are entering another waiting period. These alternating times of waiting and action have been unplanned, yet I see in them a gracious rhythm. They feel like pauses in a symphony.

Meanwhile, the work of the church goes on. James Farmer is dying. He's ready to release the burden of his schizophrenia. For thirty-six years this teacher of English has struggled courageously with his illness, knowing a measure of inner freedom only when he is in the classroom.

Other pastoral events pull me back into the daily round of congregational life. They are the constant. I like feeling grounded by the tangible things to do during these days of uncertainty.

FEBRUARY 15, 1992

From the many letters, this one is worth noting in the journal. A local lesbian psychotherapist expresses her appreciation for our willingness "to recognize the spiritual significance of lesbian and gay couples through the celebration of Holy Union." She continues:

> In my practice, I regularly encounter lesbian and gay individuals who have internalized negative self-worth beliefs related to years of religious indoctrination that homosexuals are in need of spiritual forgiveness for their sexual orientation. To repair the self-esteem of one who has been so devalued in the name of religion for so many years is almost impossible.

She went on to illustrate the church's rejection of a lesbian client—"one of the most Christ-spirited people she had known"—who died of cancer last November.

In my return letter of appreciation, I remind her that we do not know what decisions will come from the congregation. We will in twelve days. Perhaps she is responding to the significance of an open conversation.

FEBRUARY 18, 1992

When Andy and Helen asked me to meet them for coffee at the hospital dining room, I knew what to expect. I have dreaded this moment for months.

"Mahan, this is hard to say, but Helen and I are leaving Pullen." Andy tells me directly with few words, much as he might tell one of his patients that death is imminent. I tried but couldn't hold back the tears. They couldn't either.

No couple at Pullen has been more supportive through the years. Some history with Helen's brother before we came to Pullen gave our friendship a head start. We have shared so much—numerous social events, parenting challenges with children the same age, intellectual curiosities, sporting events, and similar concerns for the community.

But during the past few years they have declined leadership roles. While attending worship regularly, their drift toward the edge of the congregation has been noticeable. Pullen's direction in a number of areas has been increasingly uncomfortable to them.

"Uncomfortable" is their word. "It has become too uncomfortable for Helen and me at Pullen," Andy said. The current discussion about the gay union is part of their discomfort, but not its source. For several years they have been uncomfortable with the fundamentalist direction of Southern Baptists and have asked that we leave the denomination. Also, our current process in their judgment has been too hurried. Considering a same-gender ceremony needed more time. Andy admits, "We have stayed this long because of our friendship and we are unwilling to do that any longer."

Their decision has been thoughtfully made. Further probing of their reasons would be futile and inappropriate. These moments are painful and awkward for all three of us. I thank them for being so straightforward and leave quickly.

FEBRUARY 19, 1992

I have been thinking about my conversation with Helen and Andy yesterday morning. I can't imagine the friendship ever recovering its depth.

Yet I do admire the integrity in our exchange yesterday morning. All
three of us are placing core convictions over accommodation and avoid-
ance, even over friendship. Andy and Helen are not lost to the larger
church. As persons of faith, they will continue to serve this Raleigh community. The current discussion at Pullen challenged them to make explicit
some basic commitments that had been forming for some time. My head
goes one direction, my heart another.

FEBRUARY 20, 1992

Prophets appear at the right times. In this week's newsletter, Virginia, a
respected lay leader, names and confronts the seduction of self-righteous
pride among us:

> The Town Meeting a few weeks ago was a moving and loving experience.
> There was a strong sense of acceptance of all the feelings expressed and a
> wonderful sense of loving community.
>
> There was, however, one nagging undercurrent which concerns me. It is
> the often expressed reiteration of that old pride in our "uniqueness.". . . So,
> I am concerned when I hear people say, "This is the only place I could ever
> worship," or "This is the *only* church." What are we saying to our children,
> who may grow up and move away, or to the college student here for a few
> years, or any other folks who know that Raleigh is not their final destination
> on this earth?
>
> There is life after Pullen and we must affirm the universal church and
> family of faith. I will admit that we are special, but there are many other spe-
> cial churches not necessarily bound by denominational links. We are
> enriched by those who come to us from other places and other traditions.
> Let us not get caught up in the arrogance of "We are Number One!" Rather,
> let us trust in the Love that will not let us go.

FEBRUARY 22, 1992

I find this interesting. I talked today with Dave, a gay non-member who
comes to Pullen occasionally. Dave, and he says he speaks for others, affirms

our stand for openness, but stops short of supporting our emphasis on covenant relationships. Marriage is to him an oppressive institution. He resists the overlay upon gays of this traditional norm for heterosexuals. Some assume that the gay "community" is totally behind Pullen's consideration of a same-sex union. Dave demolishes that assumption.

FEBRUARY 24, 1992

The debate continues within me.

Could we have avoided taking a congregational vote? Doesn't a vote inevitably polarize the congregation, creating winners and losers? Does a vote on this request oversimplify a very complex question? Doesn't voting enhance either/or kind of thinking?

Yet, as some argue, would the congregation seriously study and discuss our ministry with gay Christians without a specific request that demanded a considered response? The first year of Open Forum drew a total of fifty or sixty members that included very few leaders of the congregation. It is unlikely that a large portion of the congregation would engage this question without a decision to be made.

The wisdom of voting on this request will be debated for years to come. The fact is, we have voted to vote. On Sunday the results will be known.

FEBRUARY 26, 1992

I have always liked the story about daily provision for the Israelites during their wilderness journey. Just enough "manna" is provided for a day's nourishment. Well, some manna comes today in the form of a prayer/poem by the Trappist monk, Thomas Merton. It's a gift from Joe, a close friend of our daughter, who must be reading my mind. These lines particularly speak:

My Lord God,
I have no idea where I am going.
I do not see the road ahead of me.
I cannot know for certain where it will end.
Nor do I really know myself, and the fact that I think that I am following
Your will does not mean that I am actually doing so.
But I believe that the desire to please you does in fact please you.
And I hope I have that desire in all that I am doing . . .

FEBRUARY 27, 1992

The waiting tonight is almost unbearable. I am in my office trying to write a newsletter article while the deacons are downstairs tabulating the ballots. An hour passes. Then another thirty minutes. "Why are they taking so long?"

Eventually I step into the library just as they are concluding their meeting. I could tell by Pat Long's face that the tabulation pleased her. Jim read the results. Every ear is attuned to the voting on the third recommendation—64 percent in favor of the same-gender ceremony.

Restraint is difficult. There are deacons present who are both pleased and displeased with the outcome. Quickly everyone collects their papers, reach for their coats, and leave, I suspect in search of safer places to feel what they feel.

Two-thirds seems decisive, certainly exceeding my prediction. What a relief. What would we have done with a split vote?

FEBRUARY 28, 1992

For these few days, the six of us hold this information. The results of the vote remain our secret.

This gives me time to absorb the outcome: 98 percent for the general statement of our ministry of reconciliation; 94 percent in favor of membership without regard to sexual orientation; 75 percent for a task force to articulate the biblical, historical, and theological foundation to a same-gender ceremony; and, of course, the hot-button result, 64 percent in support of the blessing on a gay union. At the conclusion of worship this Sunday Jim will announce the outcome of the vote.

On Sunday the storm returns. Jim and I are bracing for the next wave of media attention and public reaction. Today we work on the press release, review our roles and anticipate the likely responses from members and community, including the media. The relief of last night doesn't last long.

Charles McMillan of the Raleigh Baptist Association calls today. After inquiring about my welfare, he got to his point. "Mahan, if the church votes for the gay union, there will likely be a move against Pullen within the [Raleigh Baptist] Association." He means a formal break, a dis-association.

Neither Charles nor I can put on the brakes and avoid the consequences already in motion. Even if the vote were against the same-gender union, the strong affirmation of gay Christians would be enough to fuel the movement against us. Charles is an esteemed pastor to pastors, but he cannot prevent the collision of our two institutions.

FEBRUARY 29, 1992

I worry about the 177 members who opposed the ceremony. How will they respond to the news tomorrow?

Ninety-four percent of the congregation affirms the welcome of gays into full membership of the church. That's almost unanimous. Of the four decisions, it's the clearest and most important decision made. With that position unquestioned, perhaps most of us will disagree amicably about the ritual of same-gender union. I hope.

Tomorrow the curtain goes up on the next scene in this drama.

CHAPTER 9

The Hurricane's Backside

March 1–27, 1992

MARCH 1, 1992

A T THE CLOSE OF THE WORSHIP SERVICE, Jim, as moderator, sets the stage for announcing the vote by reading a statement from Bernie Cochran, a respected member for over thirty years. Regardless of the voting outcome, Bernie challenges the "congregation to treat with respect and appreciation the views of many close friends who differ on the logistics of the question before us, but whose loyalty and contribution to Pullen is lifelong and profound."

Next Jim shares a portion of his statement prepared for the media:

The heritage of Pullen inspires this church, in the spirit of Christ, to risk addressing the sometimes unconventional yearnings for healing and responsible freedoms in our day. In that Spirit, the congregation has responded to the request of one of its members by fostering a prayful and respectful dialogue as the context for determining the best sense of God's will. . . . I affirm the congregation for our capacity and courage to address openly and honestly a controversial request.

Then Jim reports the results of the voting on the four motions. I feel as if I am among five hundred family members huddled for hours in a waiting room, and finally about to hear from the surgeon the results of an operation. Jim's words seem to fall into a silent chasm.

Faces register visceral responses—delight, shock, surprise, dismay. While honoring Jim's request for no emotional outbursts, unrestrained whispering and touching cannot be restrained. Beneath it all I think I sense a collective sigh of relief: "At last a decision has been made. Can we get back to normal now?" Normality will elude us for some time, I suspect.

The word will go out today that Pullen congregation has decided to affirm gay unions, but Jim and I know better. Internally the vote is decisive, but far from unanimous. A sizeable minority, 36 percent in fact, have voted against the request from Eric and Ron. These members are in a difficult place. The church's decision that is being declared is a decision they oppose.

The TV cameras and reporters, waiting on the front steps, receive the rehearsed responses from Jim and me. We can control, to some degree, the official word, but we have absolutely no influence on comments from members as they stream from the church. The cameramen and reporters rush to them for spontaneous reactions.

Today's events call us back on stage before the public eye. The backside of the hurricane has hit, bringing to an abrupt end the relative calm of these past weeks. The front side of the storm was a shock in early January. "We have backed into a whirlwind" was my metaphor then. In contrast, this time we are not surprised. We expected the storm to return with fury.

MARCH 2, 1992

Already the reactions are reverberating with resounding "yeas" and "nays."

The results of the vote appeared on the evening news last night and on the front page of the *Raleigh N&O* this morning. The Associated Press picked up the story, passing it along to papers throughout the country, including the *Washington Post,* the *New York Times,* the *Chicago Tribune,* and the *Houston Post.*

Just as I had anticipated, the news focuses on the same-gender ceremony. I see no reference to the almost unanimous welcome of gays into full membership of the congregation. This is the headline I wish had been written: "Pullen welcomes the presence and contributions of gay Christians." Predictably, the controversy around the ceremony carries more news appeal.

In contrast to the more local reaction in January, now many responses are coming from beyond Raleigh. Newspaper reporters from Greensboro, Atlanta, Winston-Salem Washington, D.C., and Melinda Pencava, reporter from National Public Radio, call for interviews. Ferrell Guillory, from the *Raleigh News and Observer,* requests an interview for an article assigned to him by the *New York Times.*

Why this nationwide attention? The intrigue, I'm guessing, stems from two primary sources. One, an entire congregation, not just a pastor or bishop or theologian, has spoken. And two, this congregation is a Baptist church in the South.

For most people, Pullen *suddenly* decided to affirm a same-gender union. Lost in their awareness is the history behind this monumental decision. Since 1986 the church's response to homosexuality has been a part of our conversation, and increasingly during these years, gays have found at Pullen a safe, accepting community. If Eric and Ron had not made their request, some other gay couple would probably have come forward with the same request within the next few years.

MARCH 3, 1992

Phone calls have been coming at a pace that Alice can barely handle. She has learned to remain remarkably calm amid the extreme messages that range from "You tell that pastor he's going to hell" to "Please pass on to Pullen leaders my appreciation and prayers." Alice, for a second time, is the point person, the first responder.

The letters are beginning to arrive. One today was particularly direct. A former Pullen member wrote from Waco, Texas:

> I am appalled, ashamed, and embarrassed that my home church has allowed itself to be directed by such unchristian-like behavior.

Pullen's actions are even mentioned in the current issue of *USA Today.* Doris, while perusing the paper during her overnight flight from Europe, saw the brief announcement of Pullen's decision. She calls this afternoon to share the pride she felt.

I met with Ron and Eric this afternoon. The date for their ceremony—Sunday afternoon, March 15. This is really going to happen. They can't believe it. They show the excitement of any couple soon to be married. Maybe more so.

Within Pullen I feel the pulls of opposite forces, the centrifugal pull from the center outwards, spinning us out of control and the centripetal pull from chaos toward a stabilizing center that holds. The media attention

and most conversations beyond Pullen are centrifugal forces that accentu-
ate controversy. In contrast, Jim and I are leaning into the centripetal pull
toward a unifying center. The weekly newsletter continues to be an important way we can influence, however slightly, these forces.

In my newsletter column this week I call attention to the "other votes,"
so easily obscured by the attention to the same—gender ceremony. In particular, I lift up our near unanimous decision to welcome persons regardless of sexual orientation," as the most significant decision from my point
of view. We made explicit an acceptance that has been implicit for many
years.

I also remind the congregation of those members who voted their conscience in opposing the ceremony. I appeal for sensitivity to their position.
They are unable to defend a decision made by the majority at a time when
the media defines Pullen by that very decision.

I also highlight our process:

> I wrote at the beginning of our congregation discussion that the *way* we
> decide will be as important as *what* we decide. Many of us have experienced
> church in such a powerful way. The examples of courage, the honest soul-
> searching, the concern for Pullen, the openness to learning have been
> remarkable. The dual appreciation for individual responsibility and respect
> for the other will serve us well in future decision-making.

MARCH 4, 1992

Buddy Logan re-entered my life today. He called this morning from San
Francisco. He's truly a voice from my distant past. Our friendship began
during seminary years, and a few years later, we were groomsmen in each
other's wedding. However, there has been no contact for over twenty years.
He read about our decision in his local paper.

His opening words: "Mahan, how in the world did you get into all of
this?" I pick up glee in his voice. After a short answer, I reverse the question: "How in the world did you end up in San Francisco?"

He tells his unimaginable story. Fourteen years ago, he was a professor at
a Baptist college in the south when someone "outs" him as homosexual.
Within hours Buddy is fired, his ordination invalidated, and his wife and
two children demand his exit. He stumbles to Atlanta, sinks into severe

depression, and proceeds to numb his losses with alcohol. Severed from his denominational home, Buddy eventually finds a faith family in the Metropolitan Community Church and currently serves in San Francisco as pastor in this predominately gay denomination. He is estranged from many of his family and friends, although his sister and parents remain supportive. One child, he says, does still speak to him occasionally.

I may be the only friend who knows Buddy as an effective Southern Baptist pastor and teacher. I can understand his initial delight when he called. Certainly he celebrates Pullen's affirmation of gays. But even more, I am a personal link with his past.

This morning I heard that Maurice and Anna Murphy are moving their membership. Their daughter and family also. The grandson, they report, is being ridiculed at school for going to a gay church. On the way out of town today, I stop by to see them.

When the Murphys came to Pullen four years ago, they hoped our congregation would become a strong option for progressive Southern Baptists. As influential leaders of North Carolina Baptists for over forty years, they particularly feel the brunt of the fundamentalist attempts to control our Baptist institutions.

Now the decisions announced at Pullen last Sunday totally undermine their expectations. Welcoming gays is too large of a stretch, certainly not a priority they can support. They had hoped for a different outcome. It's another loss for them, and now for us.

Rumors of members leaving are rampant. At this point, I cannot distinguish between fact and fiction, but it is safe to say that every member is raising the question: "What does it mean for me to be a member of Pullen?" The answers are forming. Most are renewing their commitment with fresh enthusiasm. Some are wavering. A few are leaving. I have no way of predicting the number.

How many "Murphy" types of visits will I be making in the next weeks? Five, ten, or more? How many exit visits can I manage emotionally?

The Alliance board meets today, the convocation is tomorrow. (The Alliance of Baptists was started five years ago as a supportive network of Southern Baptists providing an alternative response to the fundamentalist movement to control the denomination.)

I expected support from the board, but I am surprised by its intensity. The board gives Pullen's action a standing ovation. And more, the board overturns my advice to cancel the workshop on the church's response to homosexuality that Pat Long and I were scheduled to offer. With the enormous media attention we are receiving, I fear the workshop being a lighting rod that would distract from and sabotage our fifth-year celebration. The board, however, after vigorous discussion, rebuffs my protective instincts, essentially saying: "No, don't cancel the workshop. We are in trouble when concerns for survival supercede our mission."

Their response is not a vote of approval for Pullen's decisions. Rather they are affirming the Alliance as a community that addresses challenging justice concerns. Then the board proceeds to appoint a task force on human sexuality with a particular focus on the church and homosexuality.

The board understands the South African saying: "When the car moves, the dogs bark. Dogs don't bark at still cars."

MARCH 6, 1992

In yesterday's mail comes a welcome gift. John Jackson, a former Sunday School teacher from university years, sends Thomas Keating's book, *Open Mind, Open Heart*. On Monday he read in the *Nashville Tennessean* about Pullen's decisions and correctly intuits my need. How did he know about the thinness of my praying, not sufficiently deep for the encounters of these days? Father Keating, a Trappist monk, is reclaiming the contemplative tradition of western Cristianity through a practice he calls Centering Prayer.

It's his focus on *letting go* that appeals. I am so wanting to let go of my over-analyzing, my fears of irreparable damage, my attachment to outcomes, my stubborn need to be understood. Keating offers a *practice,* not mere insight. During the meditation thoughts and feelings, even insights, are acknowledged, then released. Over and over again, relinquishing and returning to an inner quiet, a "resting in God's grace," to use his phrase.

MARCH 7, 1992

I'm back home from the Alliance Convocation with a sermon to finish. A knock at the door interrupts my writing. Jim Fuller, after introducing himself as chairman of the Human Relations Commission of Wake County, hands me a letter of commendation for Pullen's action. "The Commission will be present in your service tomorrow as a way of giving visible support," he adds.

More manna. Just enough sustenance for next steps keeps showing up at the door, so to speak. This action of Jim's Commission, the affirmation of the Alliance board, embraces from Alliance friends, and the gift from John—they all taste like manna to me.

MARCH 8, 1992

Today, the first Sunday since the voting results were announced. Surely it has been more than seven days. Seven years maybe?

This day will be remembered as "picketing Sunday." About eight to ten picketers gather on the sidewalk across from the church this morning. The banners display colorful declarations of God's judgement against homosexuals and Pullen. Examples: "God created Adam and Eve, not Adam and Steve." "This church is polluted. God is not here." A number of Pullen folks engage them in conversation and invite them to worship with us.

To be picketed is unsettling. It's a new experience for our congregation. Probably not one of us has entered a church service with vocal protest ringing in our ears. In my opening welcome in the worship service, I reach for a bit of truthful playfulness. "Okay folks, it is our turn now. Some of us have been protesters, carrying our picket signs expressing our support for social causes. Today we get to be on the other side."

MARCH 9, 1992

Another story from the picketing yesterday. I hear that Lori intentionally exposed her children to the picketers. She seized the opportunity for them to experience the resistance that often comes with ethical stands taken. Also, she wants her children to know first-hand the freedom to protest.

MARCH 10, 1992

The letters and resolutions of both opposition and support keep coming from throughout the nation. They are about equal in number.

This supportive letter from a pastor is particularly interesting. While visiting his gay son and partner in Chicago, he notices the announcement of Pullen's action displayed prominently and proudly on the refrigerator door. He thanks us, yet stops short of signing his name.

The assumption of gays as pedophiles shows up in this letter:

> I have not been so disgusted in a long time as when I read on the front page
> of the *News and Observer* that your church approves and condones homosex-
> uality between men and if men then certainly boys—yes, if you permit what
> you are permitting you are condoning what you permit. Just pray your son
> isn't the prey of one of your approved people who will use the church as
> approving it . . . . You have set back the image and attendance of church dras-
> tically. . . . You people are now a hopeless lost cause. I hope you come to your
> senses before you destroy the word BAPTIST and the word CHURCH.

I keep asking, what button have we pushed to trigger such fierce reactions? I look at these letters from individuals, congregations and Baptist
associations throughout the nation and realize the enormous amount of
time and energy invested in their protest, especially in the resolutions. I picture the initial outrage, then a subcommittee required to create a draft, then
finally a meeting of the association or congregation to approve the resolutions. I'm baffled by their investment.

Lay leaders continue to lead. I marvel at their stamina and love for this congregation. Hilda, for one, is visiting the homebound members, listening to
their confusion and concerns. In her appeal for healing in this week's
newsletter, she claims the authority that is rightfully hers from years of
devoted service.

> The fellowship called Pullen Memorial Baptist Church has had its problems,
> ups and downs, its pain and uncertainty before. Only the intensity of this
> current pain seems different to me. . . . Mahan aptly reminds us to take a
> pledge that what happens to a new member of our church family will make
> a difference to us . . . That's why, I do believe, it hurts when I learn that one
> of our Pullen members leaves. There is separation and brokenness . . . .
>
> So how does a family deal with pain, brokenness, uncertainty? It "bears one
> another's burdens." We are told "love bears all things." It is time now for us to
> bind up our wounds and together be a healing presence to one another.
>
> Community here together is only the beginning. It is not an end in itself.
> We are here to do the works of Him who sent us, to take up Christ's unfin-
> ished work in this time and place.

MARCH 10, 1992

Richard calls and asks for time. He can come immediately, he says. We both are eager to get this encounter behind us. I assume that he is coming to tell me that they are leaving. I'm not wrong.

Richard is an articulate, forceful leader with deep convictions. He helped to plan our stately sanctuary with its stained glass portraits of Jesus, Elijah, Moses, Peter, Paul, Luke, and the Baptists William Carey and Roger Williams.

After the phone call and before he arrived, I reminisce about our history together. When I arrived in 1983, he and Martha did everything possible to welcome and orient us to Pullen and to the Raleigh community. During these nine years, we have shared many important moments, including birthdays, weddings, funerals, my installation service, plus frequent visits in their home. I cannot imagine them going to another church.

My office door is open when he arrives. He settles into the chair that Martha purchased for me a couple of years ago. We dispense with the usual awkward phase before difficult conversations. He quickly comes to the point.

Richard's words cut like a surgeon's knife. He recounts the hope he felt in my coming to Pullen. My first years were effective, he grants me. New and younger families joined. Innovative ministries were begun. Enthusiasm returned to Pullen under my leadership. Then, in his judgment, I began to get sidetracked on controversial issues, especially homosexuality. I changed. The church changed. Now, they are changing membership.

He concludes, "Pullen has done the unthinkable by affirming gay unions as legitimate expressions of marriage. I have expressed my views in private letters and public meetings. Now that the church has acted, we have no choice. We no longer belong here."

I could feel the white heat of his pain and anger beneath his measured words. Martha, I assume, did not want to experience the anguish of this encounter. This is not a time for dialogue, so I receive his words with little response. A few weeks ago I visited them in their home where dialogue did happen. But now he is announcing their decision. Neither of us is in the mood to review the good in our years together. Someday that will be possible, but not today. I thank him for coming directly to me.

I try to imagine the sorrow in Richard's decision. Here is a man who helped design the sanctuary where he has regularly worshipped for over forty-five years. He is walking away from a faith community to which he and his family have belonged for more than fifty years. But tonight I cannot stay with his grief for feeling mine.

MARCH 11, 1992

How can we provide security for Eric and Ron's covenant ceremony on Sunday? That's the question we address at tonight's meeting.

Like any excited couple, they sent out invitations to family and friends. With the word out, we assume that the media will pick it up. Others may hear about it as well. And the picketers of last Sunday, will they return? We decide tonight to employ an off-duty policeman to handle unexpected disruptions. We further agree to ask all invited guests to enter the building from the parking lot. In that way protesters will not be disruptive because they are required by law to remain across the street from the church.

How strange it is to be orchestrating a stealth operation. Never before have I planned a worship service that includes a security guard on the lookout for protesters. There's irony in this. Eric and Ron are going public with their covenant in a secret ceremony known only to family and friends. In order to come out of a closet, we are entering a closet of sorts.

Today I received a one-sentence note from Bishop John Shelby Spong. "Mahan, in the name of God, you will experience the force of evil like never before." Yes.

MARCH 12, 1992

"I like your quote in the morning's paper," Eric told me today. "I like the part where you say that you and other heterosexual members are getting a slight taste of the prejudice that gays live with all of the time. That helps."

MARCH 14, 1992

A. C. Snow tips his hat toward Pullen in his weekly *Raleigh N&O* article this morning. This is a generous gesture from one of the community's most respected citizens. Stopping short of affirming the gay ceremony, he writes: "Still, when I heard how the congregation voted, I felt a surge of pride at living in the same town with such a church. I don't think my strong feeling constituted a vote for gay rights. It was more of a vote against intolerance."

The state Baptist paper carries the story, "Pullen Memorial Endorses Union of Homosexual Partners." In my interview for the article, I use the occasion to make two points with North Carolina Baptists.

> While there were honest differences regarding the ceremony of blessing, Pullen registered very strongly the affirmation of its heritage by a clear, decisive welcome to all persons regardless of sexual orientation.
>
> I see us having followed a very Baptist process. . . . The six weeks of discussion have been honest, respectful and informative with thoughtful members coming to different opinions. I'm amazed by the learning experienced, the relationships deepened and the faith convictions sharpened during this engaging process.

My pastoral letter to Pullen came out today. Jim and I thought that some concerns still before us could be best addressed in a separate open letter from me.

Periodically through the years I have written pastoral letters to the congregation. It's a leaf out of the Catholic tradition. In former pastoral letters I have addressed such topics as the use of inclusive language, capital punishment and racism. A pastoral letter allows for a singular focus. Besides, it can be read at the whim of the members and perhaps re-read. Or it can be lost in the stack entitled, "To be read later."

In this pastoral letter I comment on the following concerns: the role of the media; the rumor of Pullen being a pawn of some larger gay conspiracy; the soul-searching of a few deciding whether to remain members; and the fear that our mission will be re-directed from children, youth, heterosexual marriages and the ministries to the community. I reflect on the price we are paying for being "among the first [within the larger church] to face head-on the concerns of gay Christians."

I close with an appeal for unity:

> Remember, in the midst of our feeble and courageous efforts to be faithful to God and each other, what keeps bringing us together. It is not our strength and goodness and rightness. What keeps bringing us together and sending us forth in joy is the confession of our sin, the love of the enemy, the enveloping grace of God that delights in who we are, warts and all—and who delights in our becoming "mature persons to the measure of the stature of the fullness of Christ . . .speaking truth in love." (Ephesians 1: 13, 15 RSV)

MARCH 15, 1992

Ron and Eric's ceremony at last!

Today marks the end of an eight-month journey. What has been discussed for so long becomes this afternoon a reality. In Pullen's sanctuary at two o'clock Eric and Ron express their covenant vows in the presence of God and about two hundred family and friends. Thankfully, the reverence of this historic moment is not disrupted either by protesters or the media.

At first glance this seems to me like a traditional wedding—families in the front pew, flowers on the Communion table, organist in his place, the pastor in his robe, and a congregation gathered in joy. There is the typical excitement, anxiety, and awe that always accompanies the promise of life-long commitment.

It is a typical wedding *until* Eric and Ron walk down the aisle and stand before me. I'm facing two men, not a man and a woman. Two men both dressed in tuxedos, both wearing boutonnieres in their lapels. Two men looking at me no differently than other couples at the beginning of a wedding ceremony. In the long, full pause at the end of the processional, I'm thinking, "Mahan, how in the world did you get to this place?" The moment is surreal. Me? Here?

This is my first time to experience the blessing of a same-gender union. It is for 95 percent of the congregation. No longer am I advocating an idea. No longer are we discussing a possibility. I am, as representative of God and this congregation, blessing the covenant between two flesh and blood males, Eric and Ron. We are making history. Everyone feels it.

In my opening statement of welcome, I attempt to capture in words the uniqueness of the event:

> This service is both a sign of repentance and a sign of hope. We repent because we in the church have made it very difficult for gay men and lesbians to explore, express, and celebrate committed love. But this is also a sign of hope. The love between two men or two women can be as holy as the love between a man and a woman.

I also speak of the demonic. "Our coming and leaving though the backdoor, avoiding if possible the distractions of protesters, is a realistic reminder of the larger climate of hostility in which we gather."

The rest of the ceremony contains familiar elements—the hymn *Joyful, Joyful We Adore Thee;* the scripture passage, Colossians 3:12–17; a duet singing *The Gift of Love* based on I Corinthians 13; a reading from Anne Morrow Lindbergh's *Gift from the Sea;* my meditation; their exchange of vows to each other and with the congregation; the exchange of rings; and a closing prayer chosen by Eric.

Joy pervades this ending of a prolonged community effort. Hope reigns tonight, not only for Eric and Ron but for the others of us, both gay and straight, who value inclusive covenants with God and the church. We all seem to take a deep breath, letting in the wonder of it all.

As one person quipped after the ceremony: "Well . . . the ground didn't open up and swallow Pullen in it!"

MARCH 16, 1992

I woke up this morning to Ayres Wilson's *Raleigh N&O* article on Ron and Eric. What a total shock! I had no idea that Wilson had interviewed them. I'm furious.

Any article would have surprised me. But this article is schmaltzy, including references to their "nestling" on the love seat and "lying in bed declaring their love" and a "playful pinch on the belly." These are intimacies one would expect in a tabloid magazine. I can't imagine the *N&O* ever exposing the privacy of a heterosexual couple in this way.

And I feel betrayed by Eric and Ron. I thought we had an understanding that they would not be interviewed until there was some distance from the ceremony. Eric tells me that Wilson promised sensitivity (whatever that means) and that the article would be held until after the service yesterday. Eric admits the article "was a little much."

I see what happened. Like few couples, Eric and Ron had to wait to see if their ceremony would be permitted. After all these months, finally it is affirmed. Their joy was ripe for Wilson's picking. And he did.

Eric tells me that they had planned to write a letter of appreciation to the congregation. Now, he says, they will add an apology. But the damage is done. This *N&O* article will generate more juicy gossip throughout the Raleigh area. I'm thinking of those members hanging on by a thread. But I have to wonder, is my homophobia showing? Am I more uncomfortable reading about the intimacy between a gay couple than a heterosexual couple? Maybe, but I think I would have been offended by such an *N&O*

interview with any couple.

So I call Ted. He read the article and immediately understood my need: "Let's get out of town. I need some distance. Can you manage a day and night in the mountains? Some hiking might help. I just can't face the calls about this."

MARCH 17, 1992

What a mood swing. The ceremony on Sunday afternoon is an emotional, spiritual high. Celebration, relief and gratefulness mark this ending of a long journey. But yesterday I plummeted to my lowest point yet. The article felt like a hand grenade I didn't see coming. Today a measure of equilibrium is returning.

The mountains invite me to think in terms of generations. The larger church will eventually confirm or correct what we have done. We don't have to be right because truth will eventually have its way. As one pastor said to me some weeks ago, "What Pullen has done will be widely practiced in fifty years." I think Ed is right. I believe that same-gender ceremonies will be celebrated in churches and synagogues in fifty, even forty or thirty years, maybe much sooner.

But I'm still anxious. I return to conversations I dread. Highlighting the sensual, romantic aspect of Ron and Eric's relationship still feels sensational and certainly untimely.

MARCH 18, 1992

Southern Baptists are turning up the heat. The local and state Baptist leaders are inundated with calls and letters saying, "What are you going to do about Pullen?" Venting their disagreements about Pullen is not sufficient to satisfy the protest. "Expel Pullen" is the message to leaders.

MARCH 19, 1992

Ned and Carrie agree to talk with me. They are among the ones leaving, I'm told. Their twins, Janice and Matt, regularly bring one of their toys on Sunday to show me at the conclusion of worship. I ache at the thought of their absence.

Ned, usually so gifted with words, admits being speechless about homosexuality. "Mahan, I wish I could tell you why I am so opposed to the congregation's action. I just can't. I'm uncomfortable with it. It's a mistake, I believe." My efforts to draw him out are futile. He wants to talk but can't. What is within him, too deep for words?

Carrie is more articulate, less stymied. "The gay union seems permissive to me. Are there no standards? Where does Pullen say a clear 'no' to society?"

"That's precisely what we are saying," I say defensively. "I see us saying 'no' to promiscuity and 'yes' to committed love." She's not convinced. She sees us yielding uncritically to the rising gay political voice in our society.

The twins are her greater concern. What difference will this church decision make on the environment for youth? The statement behind the question seems to be: "I don't want to risk placing Matt and Janice within the influence of homosexual members and, God forbid, gay teachers. They might encourage sexual experimentation."

I feel particularly close to this family. I so want them to stay, but doubt if they will or can.

MARCH 21, 1992

Wayne Oates calls again this morning. "Checking in," he says. "I want to know how you are doing and how the church is doing." We talk about this for a while.

Then he leaves this parting word: "Well, I hope you are as concerned about committed relationships among heterosexuals as you are among homosexuals." From my beloved professor I feel a slight rebuke in his tone of voice.

MARCH 22, 1992

No picketers out front today, thank God. And I heard only a few references to the awful article about Eric and Ron in the *Raleigh N &O* last Monday. The worship felt solid. There was ground under our feet today.

The Lenten journey continues to offer a reference point. The movement of Jesus toward Golgotha and beyond provides a frame for our collective experience. Regardless of where we stand in the midst of this change, we all are feeling grief, experiencing pain, a death of what was. We can find ourselves reflected in all of the human reactions in the Passion narrative. And we know how the story ends— resurrection, life out of death, renewal from loss, grace in failure, hope from doubt, presence out of absence.

MARCH 23, 1992

Eric does as he promised. His open letter to the congregation is a good effort at addressing the concerns of the congregation. He wrote from his heart.

> Ron and I are extremely angry about the article, which we feel made us into caricatures of our true selves and sensationalized the entire process. What we wanted to come through was the love and commitment we felt for each other and the need for this to be expressed in worship, but instead the article turned into something that did not belong in the paper.
>
> We are also deeply pained by the difficulty and anxiety that this has caused for members of Pullen.
>
> In granting the interview our aim was to make things better. I am sorry for the pain it caused, pain that I share. I pray things will return to normal as soon as possible.

MARCH 23, 1992

Donna Seese has an article in the *Raleigh N&O* about the Raleigh Baptist Association sponsored forum for this Saturday at Meredith College. As a response to our decision to bless a same-gender ceremony, the Mutual Care Commission has invited each association church to send the pastor and one lay person. In her article she quotes Charles McMillan, "At this point we're just going to listen to each other. We'll wait till that's over to decide where to go from there." My comments are similar: "My hope is that our experience will not be just a source of polarization, but of dialogue and learning."

I have never received so many promises of prayer. "Know that I am praying for you and the church," comes from the known and unknown. To Kay's comment, "I am praying for you," I heard myself say, "Prayer may be why we are standing and doing so well."

Could it be that I and other leaders are standing because so many, through their "praying for you" or "thinking of you during this time," are standing with us against the lure of fear? Are we so marvelously interconnected that their compassion flows through invisible circuits? Does their love strengthen and personalize the presence of God in some way? There is mystery here.

MARCH 25, 1992

Joan comes by the office to tell me that she and Leon are leaving. "Here in this congregation our children were reared. Here we have worshipped long before your coming." She acknowledges with appreciation the help I once gave to her adult daughter, but rushes on to document their current displeasure. The church, she feels, has been taken from her.

She makes a request: "I have put my feelings in a letter. I would like for it to go into the church newsletter. I want the church to know how some of us are feeling as we leave."

I assure her it will.

There is goodness at work! After my disheartening conversation with Joan, I walk across the street to join Martin for lunch. He and Ella are always present in worship and only moderately involved in the other aspects of Pullen's life. I have no idea why he invited me.

Martin quickly relieves my anxiety. "I want you to know if Pullen had not affirmed the gay ceremony, Ella and I would have left. With some members leaving, we thought you ought to know our stance. For years I have known and worked with some wonderful persons who happened to be gay. There is no question in our mind that our church did the right thing."

He illustrates the less vocal segment of the congregation. How many, like Martin and Ella, would be leaving if we had voted against the request? That's a new thought.

MARCH 26, 1992

The leaders of the state convention have moved from disapproval to ouster. The top six Baptist leaders have recommended that any church condoning homosexuality be barred from the state organization.

Vice-President Ed Vick, speaking for the group, said, "We felt we needed to provide some leadership to show Baptists in North Carolina do not accept homosexuality as an acceptable Christian lifestyle."

I'm quoted in the article as saying, "I grieve over sending this Baptist message of rejection to persons unavoidably homosexual in sexual orientation who desire to live responsible Christian lives."

MARCH 27, 1992

With the congregation, I mourn the loss of what used to be but no longer is. Each Sunday we look around for those not present, asking ourselves: "Are they on vacation or are they too leaving Pullen? Are they on some business trip or are they visiting another congregation?"

It looks like around twenty families are leaving Pullen. Many of these members are willing to have an "exit" interview. In visits I review with them their overall Pullen experience, give thanks for the good and bless their move to another congregation. Each visit exhausts me. It's the hardest pastoral work I have ever done. But I see the end of these visits in sight.

I'm discovering that people don't leave a congregation for one reason. The recent decisions pushed most of these members over a line, but their dissatisfaction is not new. The church was on a path they could not follow with enthusiasm. And it helps me greatly to remember that these members are not lost to the church. We are not the only "show" in town. Most of these members leaving us will make strong contributions to the churches they are joining. I predict many will be happier.

And each Sunday we see new faces present for the first time.

CHAPTER 10

The Storm Subsiding

March 28–April 17, 1992

MARCH 28, 1992

WELL, IT IS A GOOD TRY. The open discussion sponsored by the Raleigh Baptist Association's Mutual Care Commission at Meredith is an effort to bring an understanding of differences. Each member church was invited to send two representatives to discuss with a few of us from Pullen the process behind our decisions. About 80 attend.

Silas Foster, the leader of the Commission with whom I met in January, presides at the discussion. He is able to sustain a civil climate in which some respectful listening occurs. Our presentation includes Mike Watts. He voted against the ceremony yet values our process.

I didn't expect any conversions. Nobody did. Mutual understanding was our stated goal. Deeper than understanding lies an unarticulated question, "Will our differences make partnership impossible?" The ties that bind us will stretch only so far. For some Baptist leaders in the Association, the ties have already snapped. As many as 27 congregations are threatening to split from the Association. "Either Pullen goes or we go," they are saying to Charles.

APRIL 3, 1992

John called last night and asked me if he could see me for a few minutes following the worship service today. With his AIDS far advanced, I am surprised that he would have the energy to travel from Durham. His mother told me recently that pneumonia is in its early stages.

John is waiting for me in my office after the service. His physical exhaustion shows. He's drawing on reserves.

Quickly John gets to the point of his visit. "Dr. Siler, I want to express my gratitude. You and the church will never know what your stand has meant to so many of us. You can't see us but we are there. I didn't want to die without you knowing this from me."

What could I say? Further words felt irreverent. I pull John from his chair. It was a long embrace.

Joan's article, the one I promised to include in the next newsletter, came out today. In the article she laments a quick resolution to a complex question. "It may be 500 years before those who evaluated cultural trends determine the better decision [about gay unions]." She speaks for herself and other older members "who have given an untold amount of love, hundreds of hours of service, and thousands of dollars; whose children were born, dedicated, baptized, graduated, and married within the love of this church." She ends her article:

> A decision to leave the church to which one has belonged for forty years or more is not entered into lightly. It is reached with many tears and with prayerful soul-searching. Whether the test of time proves this policy to be right or wrong, the effect of this vote on many of the longtime members is cruel.
>
> Dear Pullen, in your fantasy that you can be all things to all people, you have purged many who loved you most of all.
>
> Joan Boyd, with the advice and approval of others.

The letter devastates me. She reminds me why I will never feel totally good about what we have done. My thinking is clear on the matter. Our witness has been a light to so many. But could we have proceeded in a way to keep the Joan in the circle?

John and Joan put faces to the promise and cost of our actions. I remember saying to the deacons in January, "I have never felt such joy and pain *simultaneously.*" That remains the best self-awareness I can muster.

Ken, a representative of our Raleigh Baptist Association, attended our regular deacon's meeting tonight. He is in a difficult spot. While he disagrees with our decisions, he would never lead the charge for the local Association to boot us out. But the showdown is coming, like it or not. There's a rising demand for a called meeting to determine Pullen's membership.

It took courage for Ken to come and inform the deacons of what is about to happen. He raises the option: "Pullen could withdraw voluntarily from the Association and avert the public dismissal that's almost certain."

I was thinking of the counsel from a retired pastor only this morning: "Take the moral high road, Mahan. Why don't you all just pull out and not give the angry opposition the pleasure of kicking you out?"

If the decision were left to me, I might yield to the suggestion of my retired friend. Ken would like "to settle out of court." I don't blame him.

Once again, the deacons show their strength. Our membership within the Association is not in question by us. The question is being raised by the Association. In effect, the deacons are saying that we will not relieve the Association of its anxiety nor responsibility to speak their collective mind regarding Pullen's actions about homosexuality. "We have acted by the light given to us," I heard in their words to Ken. "Now, you act by the light given to you."

April 6, 1992

Editor Gene Puckett at the state Baptist paper continues to be inundated with e-mails, letters, and telephone calls. By a margin of 20–1 the messages are against Pullen. In his words, "I haven't seen anything like this in my 34 years."

Once again in his editorial this week, he laments the damage to the "larger family of Baptists."

> While sincerity and compassion for all peoples, homosexuals included, are to be commended, the decision of Pullen church did not demonstrate a loving and caring attitude toward the larger family of Baptists. It has hurt us all, creating more polarization at the very time we needed less, and prompting debates rooted in fine points of whether homosexuality is genetic or learned behavior or both.

April 7, 1992

The public witness to our story is easier for me to enjoy these days. The critical, condemning letters and calls are diminishing. There is more response coming from around the nation that expresses gratitude for the hope found in our process and decisions. What we intended to be a private conversation within a single congregation has provoked other conversations beyond our wildest imaginings.

I appreciate Larry Coleman's article. Larry, pastor of First Baptist Church in Laurinburg, made a bold, vulnerable response in his church newsletter:

> There isn't much the homosexual can do to change his/her state of being. However, there is much I must do in my own life to become a person who responds from grace rather than fear or anger . . . . I know there is a segment of the population to whom I am unable to bear witness of the gospel, not because of their sin, but because of my weakness and the struggle within me to accept persons where they are.

Larry is taking quite a risk. These words, I predict, will cost him.

APRIL 8, 1992

How's this for solidarity! During this past month we have received checks, totaling about $1,100, from unknown friends across the country. They assume correctly that we are losing some money from members choosing to leave. They want to help counter our financial losses. One of these contributors I know well: Anita Binkley, a friend from young adult days, sent a check for $400. Except for a school reunion in 1986, I haven't seen Anita for 36 years. Still more manna.

APRIL 9, 1992

In my *Pullenews* article today I alerted the congregation to the terminal condition of our relationship with Southern Baptists. I don't want them to be surprised. Since the deacons declined to recommend withdrawing from the Association, the movement toward ejection has picked up steam. A parallel movement is occurring on the state and national level. My words include:

> As painful as losing the [Southern Baptist] connection would be, it is imperative that we continue to define ourselves and not let other people or relationships do this for us. We have to keep examining and maintaining who we are in the midst of stress as well as success. . . . Inaccurately, we are accused of blessing homosexuality. As I see it, we have not blessed homosexuality any

more than heterosexuality. Ninety-four percent of us voted to welcome persons regardless of sexual orientation. Two-thirds of us voted to bless a monogamous, lifelong commitment of love between two homosexuals, much in the way we bless such covenants between heterosexuals. Exploitative, casual, uncommitted homosexual and heterosexual sexual behavior we would not bless.

APRIL 10, 1992

I am weary from being on high alert. The return to the ordinary is a welcome change. The stress is diminishing. The structures and relationships are holding. Barbara Volk, a well-respected and experienced member, has agreed to be chair of deacons this year. Conversations around the congregation are less focused on the gay union and its implications. I'm talking with fewer persons about leaving Pullen. Letters in the *Raleigh N&O* are infrequent, though the Baptist outcry continues. And, most of all, Sunday by Sunday, with the aftershocks still felt, we come together to worship God. It's our gathering, feeding place.

APRIL 11, 1992

Vickie Covington in a *Birmingham News* article commends the grace in our decision. Then she adds an insightful observation.

> The irony of all this, of course, is that there is probably no group in America today any more spiritual than the gay community. They are dealing daily with death—and its serendipity of love, friendship, and wisdom. For more than a decade they have struggled—with courage and dignity—to cope with an epidemic unlike anything this country has ever experienced.

APRIL 12, 1992

"I hear that Dick died," Nanette says over the phone in her usual crisp voice.

"Yes," I said, "I am working on his memorial service now. His service is tomorrow morning at 10:00."

"Well, I want you to know that I am still at Pullen church because of Dick."

Nanette continues to tell me that Dick always sat just in front of her each Sunday morning. Before and after the worship service they would tease each other, and in their more serious moments, they talked about their first love —flowers. Dick is the first gay friend in her life.

Once again this truth resounds: when homosexuality becomes a person and no longer an issue, conversion usually begins.

APRIL 15, 1992

It's Good Friday again. Each year I ponder what I regard as Jesus' most defining prayer: "Abba, forgive them for they know not what they do." In light of our controversy, I'm hearing it differently this year.

"They know not what they do." Ignorance does play a prominent role in the hostile reaction to homosexuals. Likely, the opponent does not know of the intense, prolonged and unsuccessful struggle of many gays who attempt to change their sexuality. They do not know the beauty of those who happen to be oriented differently from them. They do not know the loneliness of living in a "closet," constantly afraid of recognition. Neither do they know the courage it takes to "come out" as a homosexual. They do not know that for most same-sex persons their orientation is more discovered than chosen. They likely do not know the core shame from internalized condemnation from the church. They do not know that a Christian whom they respect may well be a homosexual or a parent of a gay child. Likely, the "enemies" of homosexuals do not know the roots of their own fear.

And how ignorant I was. Until I learned from the stories of gays, I did not know the impact of my youthful faggot jokes. I had no grasp of the suffering that gays endure. I knew nothing of the distinction between sexual orientation and sexual behavior. I believed that homosexual persons were deviant and devious. I did not know better.

During this Lent I am wondering what I still do not know. How could I ever know what the homosexual person experiences? During these past months I have ricocheted from one person to another, one family to another dealing with their thoughts and feelings about our process, then finally our decisions. Do I know them? Do I understand their actions? Can I comprehend their motivation?

For that matter, do I understand my own motivation? Do I know the source of my actions? How much has my leadership been self-serving? How much came from compassion? In truth, I know so little about myself.

"Father, forgive them and us, for we know not what we do." It's fitting, particularly this Good Friday, 1992.

APRIL 17, 1992

Easter Sunday. We collectively reached for hope today. High energy filled a sanctuary full of worshippers. The resurrection message—Life in Jesus coming out of death—reminded me, and I trust others, that we are a part of Something larger, a Love and Life that never ends. I felt more future, less past today. More perspective. More trust. The Easter word sounded particularly clear this year.

CHAPTER 11

The Parting of Ways
May 5, 1992–June 25, 1992

MAY 5, 1992

THE LONG-AWAITED, specially called meeting of the Raleigh Baptist association convened at First Baptist Church in Cary tonight. By a vote of 568 to 144, Pullen is expelled.

There is no surprise in that decision, or in the vote of 79 percent in favor of dis-fellowshipping Pullen. The thunderclap came from the *way* it happened, not *that* it happened.

Assuming that we would have some time for presentation, five of us from Pullen were prepared to speak. We gathered in the church library before the association meeting and rehearsed each part. Surely we would be given a few minutes to share Pullen's reasoning and process.

Jerry Hayner, the moderator, presides. He calls for a climate of calm and respect, but the angry messengers demand otherwise. The majority insists that Pullen be limited to three minutes.

I speak first, and as I approach the three minute mark, the hissing begins, accompanied with shouts of "sit down . . . your time is up!" Our friends from other churches in the spirit of fairness, keep appealing for more time. Each motion to extend our time fails by an overwhelming, resounding, "No!" The vote is soon taken. The meeting is over. The crowd has its way. It felt like a stoning.

I encouraged Janice not to come. But our son, Mark, drove over a hundred miles from his university to be with me. I'm thankful he did.

MAY 6, 1992

I'm thinking about the association meeting last night. I remain stunned over Pullen being limited to three minutes. Any secular court would have been more just.

I imagine that among the 1,000 participants in last night's meeting probably fifty or more are strongly homosexual in orientation. Some are married. Some are even clergy. Most are in the "closet." Then, I think about the two hundred plus who are parents and siblings of gay family members, some who are accepting of their loved ones, some who are not. One in four persons has a gay family member.

Then, I picture these messengers taking the results of the association's action back to their local congregations. I assume it will be celebrated by most pastors. I wonder about the gays and families of gays who will be worshipping in those churches that day. Will it not strike fear in their hearts?

I stand back from it all and feel the wonder of this event. I think of all this outrage over two men who want the church to bless their desire to love each other until death parts them. The majority of this association with whom Pullen has enjoyed a hundred-year history could not tolerate over three minutes of our story. I don't get it. I still don't understand the magnitude of these volcanic outbursts.

May 9, 1992

Unfaithfulness to the Bible is the stated reason for our expulsion from the association. "[Pullen] has acted contrary to the accepted biblical teaching regarding homosexual behavior." The resolution passed by the association claims only two biblical models for the expression of human sexuality, "a man and a woman united in a lifelong faithful relationship" or "singleness and celibacy."

Pat Long, drawing on her own biblical scholarship, responded.

I really had to wonder if these fellow Baptists had read the same Bible I read. By the Raleigh Baptist association's biblical correct rules, Abraham, Jacob, David, and Solomon all "expressed their sexuality" in unacceptable ways. The frequent biblical model for sexual expression was not monogamy but polygamy, where a man had as many wives as he could afford, and women were property, counted like cattle. If a man died without children, Jewish law (Deuteronomy 25) required that his younger brother perform the duty of a husband with his widowed sister-in-law, to provide offspring to his dead brother. So *obeying* biblical law effectively *prevented* monogamy in such cases. Jesus is asked about this custom in Matthew 28. He did not respond that the practice was immoral, but rather that in heaven marriage was irrelevant.

Virginia Ramey Mollenkott has identified thirteen different forms of family in the Bible, not one. The scriptural requirement in I Timothy and Titus that a bishop must be the husband of one wife certainly seems to imply that others in the early church were married more than once, whether sequentially or simultaneously. It becomes apparent that in biblical times, as in our own, the man and woman joined in an exclusively monogamous relationship for life are in the minority. And yet the association was asserting this relationship (or none at all) as the only biblical model.

MAY 21, 1992

"Strike two!" came from the state Baptist leaders yesterday. "Strike one" was the local association's vote to expel us on May 5. And "strike three!" will predictably come from the national Southern Baptist Convention in its annual session in June. Then, with three strikes, we will be completely "out" of the Southern Baptist network.

In the action yesterday by the state leaders, both Binkley Memorial Baptist (which affirmed a gay seminarian's license to preach, a first step toward ordination) and Pullen are defined as "non-cooperating" churches for taking an "official action which manifests public approval, promotion or blessing of homosexuality." The vote of the General Board of the Baptist State Convention to expel: 59 for, 28 against, with one member abstaining. Now a position on homosexuality will apparently determine "cooperation."

MAY 26, 1992

Pullen is taking a deep breath and moving on. I can feel the difference. Immediate staff transitions are claiming our attention—sending Michael Hawn and Dan Schellenberg off with our blessing and welcoming Nancy Petty as minister of education. The storm is over. Much repair work lies before us, but threats to our core identity and mission have passed. Quite the opposite, I predict that our core identity and mission will be clearer, more forceful. A wounded Pullen community is showing remarkable resilience.

JUNE 1, 1992

My lessons are not finished.

Mark and Phil joined Pullen a few months ago. I'm impressed with their maturity, and now their compassion. They have adopted Larry, an African American crack baby who had been abandoned by his mother. They are looking to Pullen for primary support as they assume this daunting responsibility.

They ask me to drop by. Soon into our conversation this morning, Phil raises the question: "When will the next parent-child dedication be at the church? Would it be okay if we take part?"

I tell them that the next dedication service would be in November. Phil continues: "We know the church is just beginning to heal and move on. If we need to wait a year, we will. We would like to participate, but we sure don't want to get the media involved."

After appreciating their sensitivity, I respond: "You are right about the ritual. It's designed for what you request. Within worship, these commitments are highlighted: your commitment to Larry and Pullen's commitment to the three of you, all within the context of our mutual commitment to God. I will check with the deacons and get back to you."

But all during this conversation, my insides are churning. Pullen has just begun to settle down from all of the controversy. Can we handle another new thing? Can we stretch any farther? When I got back to the privacy of my car, I admit letting out a Tevye-like prayer, "God, give us a break!"

I sat in the car and pictured the November event: across the front of the sanctuary five or six traditional couples standing with their children to be dedicated. With them are Mark, Phil, and young Larry—a white gay couple with an African American child in their arms.

"Beautiful," my gospel heart says. A powerful, visible witness to interracial justice, same-gender covenants, and parenting by gays. A triple play! And yes, also add the marvel of their compassion for the abandoned Larry. But my fearful heart says, "Will this be the last straw for more members?"

The deacons don't hesitate when I present the request from Mark and Phil. They do not flinch, in essence saying, "We have 'put our money down.' Let's proceed." One deacon spoke for many: "When has a couple been so deserving of our support to their parenting?"

All through this journey of gay inclusion, when I have wavered, there have been others who have stood firm. I'm remembering specific instances with Pat Long, RRNGLE (Raleigh Religious Network for Gay and Lesbian Equality), the Alliance of Baptist board, and now once again the deacons.

JUNE 10, 1992

And finally the "third strike." At last, we are "out." Yesterday the 17,900 messengers to the Southern Baptist Convention, meeting in Indianapolis, voted overwhelmingly to "withdraw fellowship" from Pullen and Binkley. They act on a recommendation from the Executive Committee that declares our two churches "not in friendly cooperation" with the SBC. As one state editor notes: "[This is] the first time that a moral issue has been used to limit membership in the 147-year-old denomination."

The action from the national body draws little attention in the media and even less in our congregation. Our ties with local and state Baptists have been important, but for years now, we have felt more dissonance than identity as a Southern Baptist congregation.

JUNE 24, 1992

One personal act of closure with Southern Baptists remains. Today I sent an open letter to the state Baptist paper *(Biblical Recorder)* and to *The Commission* (a periodical of the Christian Life Commission, Southern Baptist Convention, focusing on ethics).

In this letter I express gratitude for the gifts to me from Southern Baptists—exemplary theological education, numerous opportunities for ministry, including five Southern Baptist congregations and adjunct teaching at two seminaries, and trusteeship of two Baptist institutions. I express thanks for the enriching relationships from each of these contexts.

This is the heart of my letter:

> My parting concern is that you are making as a condition for cooperation in Christian ministry a particular position in regard to homosexuality. Your position seems to include the following *assumptions:* (1) In contrast to heterosexuality, homosexual orientation is chosen, not discovered. (2) The role of the church is to persuade homosexuals to abandon their sexual orientation or, at least, remain silent and celibate. (3) No distinction should be made between biblical condemnation of promiscuous, idolatrous homosexual behavior and homosexual intimacy within a monogamous, lifelong, committed relationship. (4) Religious and cultural violence against homosexuals is not a major social injustice against which the church should give clear prophetic witness. (5) Homosexual "lifestyle" means any expression of

homosexual behavior. (6) Being gay and Christian are incompatible identities.

You would expect me to challenge these assumptions. But more important is the creation of a climate where debate and differences of opinions are respected. In the face of this complex issue, dogmatism is unwarranted. Devout, learned Baptists disagree. I hope, within the Baptist tradition of dissent, you will support safe places for continuing dialogue in common search for the mind of Christ.

Southern Baptists will pick up this dialogue whether they want to or not, later if not sooner. This conversation is "out of the closet" and cannot be stopped.

JUNE 25, 1992

Mike Watts is the perfect choice to say last rites over the death of our 108-year relationship with Southern Baptists. Mike is a Baptist through and through who grieves more than most of us this loss of Southern Baptist identity. He voted against the ritual of blessing. He is a new deacon, a tribute to his integrity and to the desire of the congregation to value the differences among us.

In our worship service Mike leads the "Litany of Hope" that celebrates the gifts from our Southern Baptist connection, acknowledges the pain in our separation, and calls for grace in the parting of ways.
Mike concludes:

> As we part company with the Southern Baptist family, may we separate without bitterness, but with sorrow for the loss of fellowship, with love for those we leave behind, and with hope for a better future, both for Southern Baptist congregations and for Pullen.

In the service, this prayer is offered:

> O God our help in ages past, our hope for years to come. God, we have met you here in this place before. From our past we remember hearing your voice at Pullen's birth 108 years ago; during discussions about women deacons; in decade-long dialogues on race relations; during exchanges with Baptist friends over baptism and church membership; during troubled talks

about the Vietnam War. You spoke to us then, and we remember your voice.

And now, dear God, these past few months we have heard your voice again. We have heard your familiar voice in the witness of those who have recently reunited with you and the church; in the anguish of those who fear for our church family; in the joy of those with new insights; in the pain of those who feel excluded. Pardon our asking for answers, and bless our willingness to struggle to discern your truth. Thank you, God, for speaking to us then and now.

We acknowledge your voice, and we recognize your abiding presence in our lives now and forevermore. Thank you for speaking to your children at Pullen. In Jesus Christ, we pray.

Amen.

Epilogue

O N FEBRUARY 10, 2002, Pullen Memorial Baptist Church gathered to commemorate the tenth anniversary of its self-defining action that sent tremors of delight and disdain throughout the nation. The congregation wanted to recall and celebrate the months of discussion that culminated with a vote to welcome Christians who happen to be homosexual in orientation, and, in particular, to bless the union of two gay men. Now retired for almost four years, I was invited to return and share in this reflective, joyous event.

While sitting in the pew on that anniversary Sunday, listening and singing with these friends of fifteen years, I reminisced about the questions raised a decade ago.

Will this decision split the church?

For some, the question was a statement: *"Mahan, this will split the church!"* Yet, today I look around and see many faces, many new faces. The congregation is larger in size and appears to be larger in spirit. The vision of inclusion behind the church's decision has drawn new persons and families, both straight and gay.

There are those I don't see as I cast my eyes around the congregation. Even after ten years, I grieve the absence of devoted members who chose to leave this congregation. After thoughtful, respectful consideration, Pullen made a decision. So did they.

But did the congregation split? No.

Will we become a gay congregation?

Some prophesized this outcome. They feared homosexuals would storm the doors, eager to become members, with heterosexuals leaving Pullen out of discomfort. This didn't happen either. Many lesbians and gay men, bearing the wounds from a judgmental church, are still reluctant to trust a different experience. Their hurts are deep, their suspicions profound.

Yes, there are more gay couples and individuals in the congregation, but I also observe more young families. Children are plentiful, far more than ten years ago. The worship bulletin displays a full array of ministries and educational opportunities. This is not a "single-issue" church. The diversity is striking.

With the media highlighting the gay union, would the members who opposed it be respected and appreciated? Would they stay? Could they stay?

Jack McKinney, the current senior minister, in his sermon today addressed this concern:

> Those of you who disagreed with the decision, but remained in the church, have provided one of the strongest witnesses to the meaning of Christian community. Your willingness to remain engaged, to form relationships, and to keep supporting your church has been a catalyst to the deeper understanding of genuine community that has flourished here.

How would our conversation and decisions about same-gender orientation affect our relationship with other congregations, particularly other Baptist churches?

Little did we know at the time that our actions would lead to our expulsion from Southern Baptists on all three levels—local, state and national. For 108 years, Pullen had been Southern Baptist.

Many congregations did distance themselves from Pullen. Other churches, however, both Baptist and non-Baptist, moved toward us with immediate support and desire for long-term partnership. Today, ten years later, Pullen is more vitally connected with the larger church than ever before in its history.

If we adopt this ritual of blessing that affirms same-gender covenants, won't we be inundated with requests from other gay couples?

That didn't happen either. I can recall nine ceremonies for gay couples before I left in 1998. There have been three or four since then. This would be in contrast to over forty heterosexual weddings during the same ten-year period.

What will happen to Eric and Ron?

Occasionally I am still asked about them. A few months after their ceremony, Eric received a postdoctoral grant in his field of physics which took them to Washington, D.C. For the next couple of years, they would return to Pullen for brief visits. In 1996 I heard that they had separated.

This commemorative worship service was followed by a panel discussion in the fellowship hall. Pat Long, Bill Correll, and Jim Powell, who were deacons in 1992, served on the panel. I was asked to join them and also share my reflections from this ten-year perspective. For a closing statement I wished I had thought to read my final words in Pat Long's engaging account of Pullen's holy union process, *Enlarging the Circle:*

> Occasionally in the course of church ministry I have felt a keen sense of being a part of something larger—or more accurately, a part of Something larger, God, Spirit at work confronting and summoning, healing and transforming. Being a part of Pullen's decision regarding gays and gay unions has been such a time. A "kairos" time it has been, when a courage and wisdom we did not possess was given to us.
>
> But the ongoing grace of God, I hope, abides— grace for the insensitivities and mistakes, grace that undergirds and enables honest differences between us, grace stronger than the self-righteousness which comes with standing up and sticking out. Grace to us all—and peace.

SECTION II

Leading the Process

Introduction

HOW WILL WE AS A CONGREGATION RESPOND to those of same-gender orientation, both those within our church and those in our community? I imagine this question before you. You are asking, Is it time to address this situation? And if it is, how would we design and lead a process for discerning the spirit of Christ in our response?

This section is designed to be a resource for you in two ways. First, it will help you assess your readiness for this conversation. Second, it offers suggestions for leading the process. I am drawing from my knowledge of twenty congregations that have engaged in this dialogue. With six of these congregations I have served in a consulting role. With one I served as pastor.

In August 1999, following my retirement from Pullen, I helped convene representatives of thirteen congregations who had explored their relationship to gays and their families. We asked the question: *What have we learned about when and how to lead this process within a congregation?*[1]

The contours of this conversation varied from congregation to congregation. Some came to a clear affirmation of gays into full membership. Other churches stopped short of a congregational decision. Often the conversation was kept on the church's agenda, at times picked up with focused study and discussion, at other times laid aside while other concerns occupied the members' attention. A few of these congregations chose to embrace the affirmation of gay ordination and same-gender unions.

The desire for discernment also surfaced in a variety of ways. Some initial interest came from leaders, others from members. Now the question or request has come to you.

I offer five steps for you to consider as you imagine leading a process of discernment:

- readiness
- anticipating the stages
- leadership
- creating a plan
- implementing a plan.

1. The insights harvested from this retreat became the basis for my feature article in the resource, *Rightly Dividing the Word of Truth: The Congregational Response to Gay and Lesbian Persons,* edited by Le Dayne McLeese Polaski and Millard Eiland (Baptist Peace Fellowship of North America, 2001), and later in my article, "Blessings Unforeseen" in *Otherside* (Dec.–Jan. 2002).

CHAPTER 12

Readiness

L ET'S BEGIN WITH THE QUESTION OF *when*. When is the time to initiate this conversation within the congregation? Either you have been asked to consider a planned discussion on the church's response to homosexual persons or this desire has come from among yourselves as leaders. Is this the time to proceed? Consider these factors.

I. ACKNOWLEDGING THE FEAR

There are reasons that make this conversation different from other congregational discussions. First note the church's hesitancy to address the subject of sexuality. While our culture is rampant with sex talk, the church has largely kept silent. We have inherited a dualistic tradition that separates the spirit from the body, positing sexuality as inferior, if not antagonistic to spirituality.

Also, sexuality is a private matter, a subject not easily discussed in public. How we understand and express our sexuality goes to the core of our being. "Don't talk about sexual feelings" is a taboo likely learned at home and reinforced at church. And we can expect some members to harbor secrets about homosexuality. A few may be men and women of same-gender orientation in heterosexual marriages. Families often hide the fact that family members are gay or lesbian. So it is important to realize that you are considering a public discussion of a subject usually kept private.

The fears of having this discussion will be present. They go beyond the fear of change itself, always present when we are challenged to see and do differently. Facing the anxiety around this potential conversation may be the first step in readiness. Fear is generally not paralyzing when acknowledged.

Are you able to discuss your own fears about proceeding? Can you recall other anxious discussions within the congregation? How were they led? Was there sufficient safety for members to trust speaking their mind and heart?

2. Reviewing your mission

Take time to review your sense of mission. Consider the formal written documents that describe your church covenant, but reflect, as well, on the informal assumptions. What do you hear other members saying about your mission? What priorities are revealed by your budget? How would you define your purpose?

Then ask: Does an open consideration of our relationship with homosexual persons fit with our self-understanding as a church? Will this search for clarity feel congruent with the mission of our church? Does our understanding of God's intention, most clear in Jesus, draw us toward this discussion?

You are not ready until your process of discernment can be placed within the context of your mission. Seeing this exploration as discerning faithfulness to God provides the grounding and inspiration that this conversation requires.

3. The strength of relationships

The conversation you anticipate will take place within relationships formed by covenant. In response to God's promise to be with us as compassion, you have promised to be instruments of this compassion to each other and for the world. These covenants make possible a safety in which you can speak truth in love to one another.

As you evaluate your readiness, weigh the maturity of relationships, particularly between the pastor and congregation, between leaders and congregation, and among leaders. Are relationships sufficiently strong to contain and lower anxious reactivity? Will most relationships hold, not break, when differences are expressed?

The process you envision is more than a rational discourse. Feelings will also be present. Only solid relationships can provide the trust in which this challenging conversation can take place. When covenants with God and each other are reasonably strong, then the anxiety in this discussion will more easily be accepted, contained, and managed.

4. Checking for residual issues

Are there significant, festering residual issues in the congregation that might be laid on top of this conversation in a distracting or destructive manner?

Sometimes emotionally charged discussions can be contaminated, even undermined, by unresolved issues carried into the present.

Or, there may be other major concerns before the congregation at this time. A capital campaign, the adjustments to a new pastor, or the construction of a building are examples of preoccupations that could siphon off energy needed for this dialogue.

Insofar as you can detect, do you anticipate that most of the members will be free from unresolved issues carried over from the past? Will they be attentive to a planned process?

5. COUNTING THE COST

Costs occur from this conversation. What might they be?

You can expect this conversation to consume significant time and energy that could be invested in other ministries of the church. This includes additional pastoral care. More attention is required when you assume a bifocal approach: the focus on the content of the discussion, and the focus on its impact on relationships.

Openly discussing your relationship with gays will be a defining conversation. Your self-understanding as a congregation will become clearer in some way. Your relationships within and beyond the congregation are affected. Some of these changes will be experienced as loss.

The Pullen story is atypical. Approximately twenty families left this 800-member congregation, and the church was ejected from its Southern Baptist denomination. This was in 1992. Pullen was the first church in its region to define its relationship to same-gender persons through a congregational process. Furthermore, this took place at a time in Southern Baptist life when intense struggles between fundamentalist and nonfundamentalist factions engrossed the denomination. Within this denominational turbulence, the Pullen congregation became a lightning rod.

My experience with other churches engaging this question reveals a different story. In a some instances, this open discussion did jeopardize denominational connections. But even in these congregations, few members left the congregation over this discussion.

6. COUNTING THE BLESSINGS

You can anticipate blessings. Among the twenty congregations I observed not one regretted having this conversation. To the contrary, each congregation celebrated lasting benefits from the experience. Some benefits were surprising.

Churches experienced membership renewal. Because of the open discussion about being in covenant with gay Christians, each member asked, "What does it mean to be a member of this congregation?" The listening required and the convictions expressed deepened relationships and formed new ones. Most members felt a new appreciation for a community able to talk and make decisions within a context of mutual respect.

The process of discerning became an unexpected educational windfall. Vital questions of faith surfaced in the discussions: What is God's will? What would Jesus do? How do we interpret Scripture? What is the mission of our church? How can we love and differ? What does it mean to be in covenant with each other?

These congregations all reported a rejuvenation of worship life. Worship services were occasions for listening more intentionally for God's guidance. Any anxieties and questions generated by the process could be part of the weekly offering. Sunday by Sunday, preaching, liturgy, and hymns reminded members of covenants that transcend and embrace differences of conviction.

Evangelistic outreach was another surprising blessing. These churches discovered persons in their larger community looking for a faith family that honors their identity as both gay and Christian. And there were parents of gay children seeking a church that offered support. Others were looking for a safe place where struggles with sexuality and spirituality could be explored. These churches attracted still others looking for congregations willing to risk in the service of justice and compassion. They were saying, "We want to be a part of a community like that!"

Another benefit is not immediately obvious. This process of discernment will better prepare you for future conversations around other issues. You strengthen your confidence in addressing emotionally charged concerns. The content of future discussions will change; the process remains available for future challenges.

These are factors for you to weigh as you anticipate this open dialogue. No one factor should be determinative. Looking at them together will give you a sense of your readiness.

CHAPTER 13

Anticipating the Stages

HAVING REVIEWED YOUR READINESS, I picture you wondering about the process. What will it look like? What stages can we expect to face?

The "coming out" of silence by a pastor or congregation engaging the discussion of homosexuality is similar to the process of "coming out of the closet" experienced by a homosexual person.[1] At this point, you *don't* know how your congregation will decide to be in relationship with gays. You *do* know that breaking the taboo of silence with an open conversation will set you on a course of change. The stages in that change are important to identify and anticipate.

THE CLOSET OF SAFETY

For the homosexual person, the closet provides the darkness that protects against the prejudice and hatred of others. It is a safe place. Staying hidden can secure one from the threats of losing family, lifelong friends, and perhaps employment. But it is a costly place of secrecy. While a certain truth is hidden, living the lie of one's identity publicly compromises self-respect that over time often disintegrates into self-hatred.

Similarly most churches act as if homosexual persons and their families are nonexistent. The church keeping the presence of gays a faith-family secret is not to be confused with the right of privacy for gays. It is the open concern for homosexual persons and their families that remains "closeted" in most church circles.

But you are considering coming out of this closet of silence. Both the church and individual homosexuals experience a similar movement through parallel stages. These are: *confusion, listening, thinking, realignment of relationships,* and *integration.*

Stage #1: *Confusion*

When the secret is broken, usually confusion initially reigns. "Coming out" to parents or work colleagues or friends throws these relationships off balance. Even where homosexual orientation is suspected, to name this openly is disorienting. In the effort to recover balance and comfort, the lesbian or gay man may receive denial, anger, or even rejection. Clearly this new knowledge will change these relationships, but at this point, no one knows exactly how the new change will take form. The discomfort is poignant, lasting for a brief or extended time.

Expect this same period of confusion if you proceed with a planned discussion. The open conversation alone will disrupt the comfort zone of a congregation. There will be fear, likely some anger, and withdrawal in the search for relief. Members will intuit correctly that this conversation will change the balance within relationships. By anticipating this discomfort, you can name its inevitability as the first stage of a process.

Stage #2: *Listening for understanding*

A constructive next stage in the coming-out process of a gay person is listening for understanding. While honoring their own confusion, the task of parents, friends, or colleagues is to hear their story. Before opinions are formed and voiced, understanding the life experience of the openly gay person bypasses quick judgment. And the mature homosexual, coming from a self-understanding long in formation, will also be committed to listening with patience to the questions and concerns of the parent, friend, or colleague. This listening for understanding requires effort on two levels: honoring feelings and comprehending thoughts.

The stage of listening for understanding is equally imperative for the church-going public in its pursuit of clarity regarding homosexuality. This is not the time for expressed convictions. Quick opinions can polarize the congregation into camps. First, everybody's response—whatever that response may be—needs to be heard and valued. As leaders, your task at this stage is to encourage the suspension of judgment in the service of listening for understanding. (Suggestions for structuring these safe places will follow in the comments on designing a plan.)

Stage #3: *Thinking for conviction*

Likely the coming out of one who is homosexual will create the need for information. Most family and friends are confronted with an aspect of human sexuality that is outside of their experience and knowledge. Written materials and interpretations from others are available for study. At some point everybody involved must think through their responses.

Similarly, after the valuing of stories, the church will need access to information about sexual orientation. The educational aspect of this conversation rises to the surface. The study of scripture, the opinions of the church in history, and the current scientific understanding of homosexuality stimulates the thinking required for sound convictions. Imperative are safe places for members to discuss their thinking as persons of faith about the questions before the church. (Suggestions for this aspect of the conversation will be included in the section on planning and later in the bibliography.)

Stage #4: *Realignment of relationships*

After an extended time for listening and thinking, the relationships of an openly gay person will settle into a new place. The discomfort eventually yields to a new balance in being together. This resolution in relationships will settle somewhere along the continuum from rejection to acceptance.

The realignment of relationships will occur in your church experience as well. Coming from a period of listening, study, and reflection together, members will reach some conclusions. In this process, new friendships will be formed. More seasoned relationships in the church will be adjusted if not deepened. Some members may choose to join other congregations. Closeted gays may move to the edges of the congregation for fear of exposure. Others, both gay and straight, will come closer together. You can expect that this conversation, to some degree, will change the relationships within the church and beyond the congregation. Such realignments are happening all the time, but the shifts in relationships from this discussion will be more obvious.

Stage #5: *Integration*

At some point in the process of coming out, the sexual orientation of a friend or family member becomes a non-issue. This awareness is integrated as one aspect of the loved one's or colleague's life. This is true only if the relationship has moved successfully through these prior stages.

A congregation can, as well, reach a point where the same-sex orientation of church members is no longer the primary manner of identification.

What's true for heterosexuals becomes true for them. The issue of sexual orientation recedes in importance.

Reconciliation, as opposed to agreement, may be a part of this final stage. Convictions may not be reconciled, but relationships can be. Understanding and respect within mutual commitments to Christ can transcend and heal the differences over the church's response to homosexuality.

These stages, like stair steps, will characterize your process. While every person and congregation does not go though these stages in lockstep, a general movement toward integration can be anticipated. Each stage is built upon the successful completion of the previous stage. Becoming stuck at one stage is a danger signal. Regardless of the outcomes from this process, your challenge is to name, guide, and encourage the congregation through the movement from confusion to integration. Knowing and anticipating these stages will enhance your leadership.

1. Karen A. McClintock draws this same parallel in her article, "Why is Homosexuality so Hard to Talk About?" in *Congregations Talking about Homosexuality.* The stages that a homosexual person goes through in coming out becomes a way to anticipate the stages you can expect in a congregational discussion.

CHAPTER 14

Leadership

A ssuming that you want to proceed with some kind of conversation, let's turn to leadership. There are two faces to leadership of a planned dialogue: content and process.

The *content* of the discussion includes: theological perspectives; interpretation of relevant passages of Scripture; the shared questions, experiences, and convictions of members; appropriate historical and scientific data; and the wording of proposals presented to the congregation at any point in the process.

The process of the dialogue includes: how the conversations are framed and decided; how the discussions are facilitated; how the differences are handled; and how decisions are made.

Thus, effective leadership requires a bifocal vision: staying focused on the goals for the conversation while remaining focused on the people engaged in the process.

1. Leadership Team

One congregation with whom I worked developed a leadership team. I recommend that you consider this option. This team, formed for overseeing the content and process, can lift this responsibility from standing committees with other work to do.

The church that used a leadership team first asked what leadership functions were needed. They created this list:

- framing the issue theologically
- interpreting scripture and other relevant documents in church history and contemporary science
- designing an inviting process within an atmosphere of mutual respect

- facilitating group discussion
- extending pastoral care to those confused, agitated, or alienated by the process of discernment
- leading worship and prayer support
- communicating with the media and other church bodies.

Then they matched the functions with persons who could offer these aspects of leadership. Their team, consisting of ten members, met regularly to plan and shepherd the process to completion. They reported regularly to the elected leadership of the congregation and occasionally to the entire congregation.

Depending on the kind of open discussion you are considering, the functions of leadership will differ. The constituency and size of the leadership team must match your particular needs.

2. The role of pastor(s)

What will be the pastor's role in this conversation? At the outset I suggest that the pastor with the lay leaders address the question: What role will I assume? What role will I not assume?

I have observed pastors answering this question differently. All pastors influenced both the content and flow of the conversation. Some took a more active, upfront role by articulating their positions through preaching, writing, and teaching. Others focused more on an indirect role, supporting the upfront leadership of others while offering additional pastoral care as needed. Some tilted toward the prophetic task; others toward the priestly task. The pastor's role might change as the process with the congregation continues, but being intentional, clear, and consistent enables both the congregation and the pastor(s) to know what to expect.

3. Gay or lesbian leaders

Are there current leaders in your congregation who are open about their homosexual orientation? Are there mature gay members in the congregation who can be drawn into leadership roles? Do you know of respected homosexual persons outside of the church who could be called upon for counsel, if not leadership, at specific points in the process?

Without gays in leadership roles there is the risk of the conversation being about "them" rather than about "us." In the congregations I observed, having leaders of same-gender orientation was invaluable. They put a face and words to the multiple perspectives of lesbians and gay men. They are especially helpful if they can respond to questions and concerns in a nondefensive, respectful manner. Including them in the planning and implementation will strengthen the dialogue.

4. Leading from your past

You may want to include somewhere in your plan an intentional look into your church's history. Likely there are moments in your tradition that can support and perhaps inform your process.

Other churches found it useful to recall those times in their history when challenging questions were addressed. They asked: What are our memories of those times? What made these discussions constructive? How could they have been planned and led more effectively? What can we learn from those times that might help us in this conversation?

This dialogue will feel uncomfortably new to most members. To realize that unsettling challenges are a part of your history invites confidence. "We faced uncomfortable questions then and survived, even thrived. We can do it again."

5. Working with the Media

The conversation you intend for your congregation may or may not be a media event. In recent years the stories of congregations considering their relationships with persons of same-gender orientation are more common, possibly less newsworthy. In my experience, most churches became a news item either in the denominational or secular media, sometimes both. The media can be partners in communicating the church's witness to the larger community.

Be prepared for interaction with the media. The lack of preparation can send mixed messages at a time when clarity from leadership is paramount. Assume the media will want the story. If a reporter calls, don't avoid their advances. Otherwise you may lose your influence on what is reported. I urge you to be ready to shape the story you want communicated to the larger community. As you do this, realize that what the media reports will be overheard and become a part of the dialogue within your congregation.

Consider the following guidelines:

- Decide in advance which leader or leaders will speak to media for the congregation.
- If media contacts the church, spend time clarifying for yourselves what you want to communicate and what you don't.
- Craft carefully worded statements that can be given to the press, including in your words a fair representation of all sides of the issue.
- Consider the resource of coaching from those who are experienced in working with the media.

6. Use of Consultation

Leaders of the congregations in my experience made use of outside consultants including: leaders from other congregations that had experienced a similar process; professionals skilled in designing or facilitating small group discussions; specialists in biblical interpretation or the current understanding of homosexuality; process consultants who assisted in designing a plan for a congregational conversation and decision-making; denominational executives who were able to address the impact on denominational relationships; and media specialists who coached leaders on their interactions with the media.

Clarifying the leadership of the process needs to be a part of your planning. The quality of presence and competence in leaders will be the single most influential factor to the outcome of this conversation.

CHAPTER 15

Creating a Plan

EACH CONGREGATION I OBSERVED DEVELOPED a different plan for discerning their relationship with lesbians, gays, and their families. This list of components for you to consider comes from the collective experience of these congregations.

1. WHAT IS THE QUESTION?

Wherever it comes from, be clear about the question(s) around which you are planning a conversation. To be confused at this point will cause confusion at every point. Decide whether the conversation will lead to a decision by the congregation, or whether your planned discussions will stop short of specific action. Will you address one question at a time? Some congregations dealt with a question for a period of time, then backed off, only to return later to the next stage in the conversation. In contrast, other churches preferred to proceed toward specific resolutions while the energy was focussed.

Questions will vary from congregation to congregation. These are examples:

- What does the Bible say about homosexuality?
- What are other churches or denominations saying and doing about this issue?
- Will gay, lesbian, bisexual, and transgender (GLBT) persons be welcomed into full membership of our congregation?
- Will we affirm the election of GLBT persons to leadership?
- Will we consider the request for ordination from a gay member?
- Will we baptize or confirm an openly gay person?

- Will gay couples with children be included in the ritual of infant baptism or child dedication?
- Will we offer the ritual of God's blessing and the blessing of the congregation upon same-sex covenants?

2. WHAT IS THE TIME LINE?

How much time will this discussion require? In some congregations, the plan for discussion and decision-making had a precise beginning and ending because a specific request demanded it. The requests varied, including a request for church membership (individual or couple), adult baptism, infant baptism or child dedication, ordination, or a blessing of a gay union. These requests called for a specific response in a timely manner.

Most congregations in my experience were not responding to a specific request from a gay person or couple. The initiative came from leaders or members who saw this conversation as timely. They wanted the church to structure a process for discernment. In these instances the process can enjoy a measured pace without the pressure to respond to a precise request.

In either case, the time frame must be clear. Some congregations I observed began an open-ended conversation without an agreed-upon end in sight. Midway into the conversation there were those who wanted more time. And there were those who wanted closure. Neither group was satisfied. Insofar as is possible, the question of timing needs to be understood at the outset with assessments of the process built in along the way.

3. WHAT GOES INTO THE PLAN?

As you design your process, consider these six components: the sharing of stories; the study of homosexuality in the Scripture, church history and modern science; additional pastoral care; leaders of the process; congregational affirmation of the process; and evaluation of the process of discernment.

A. The sharing of stories

Every member has history with the topic of homosexuality. Persons, whether homosexual or heterosexual, have their own thoughts, questions, fears, and assumptions about this subject. Providing safe places for personal sharing and listening is the first major stage in an effective process of discernment.

These personal narratives may include: persons of same-gender orientation willing to share their stories of what it is like being homosexual in the church and our society; both heterosexuals and homosexuals willing to express their internalized messages about homosexuality; persons sharing their experiences with homosexual persons, past or present, positive or negative; church members open with their ambivalence and struggle; and parents or other family members willing to speak about their experiences of loved ones who are gay.

Putting faces on the issue and voices to the emotions invite a level of trust not achieved in any other way. This is particularly powerful when those of different sexual orientations are in conversation together. It hedges against "we" and "them" thinking.

Some stated guidelines or ground rules will foster the safety required in the sharing of stories. One is listening for understanding, not debate. Articulating differences in points of view comes later. At this early point in the public discussions, deferring judgments will enhance safety. When appropriate or needed, remind members that they gather from an unknowing stance. We will learn from each storied point of view.

The distinction between "I" and "you" messages provides guidance, as well. Encourage each person to speak with "I" messages ("I think this . . . My experience is . . .") as opposed to "you" messages ("You shouldn't feel that way; you are so right or so wrong; you always . . ."). Loving in this context means I care enough to offer you my perspective. Conversely, loving means I care enough to understand your perspective to your satisfaction. The courage to express life experiences while being open to those of others requires a high level of maturity.

There are multiple formats for storytelling in a church setting. Representative points of view can be printed in the newsletter. Stories can be shared in worship services or in less formal settings. Small group discussions in homes or at the church provide more relaxed settings. I have witnessed the effectiveness of the "fishbowl" format in which members who wish to speak are placed in an inner circle with others listening, not questioning or reacting. Perhaps the most important personal sharing occurs in informal settings after church events, along the church corridors, in the parking lot, and over the phone.

B. *The study of homosexuality and the church*

Value, as well, the intellectual component to this discernment process. Information gathering, theological thinking, biblical interpretation, and the exchanges of points of view become the next stage in the process. Consider these five aspects for study.

1. How is the Bible interpreted? This question of hermeneutics is foundational. How you view Scripture will affect the biblical guidance you find on any topic, especially homosexuality. Seldom are we pressed to clarify our assumptions about interpreting Scripture. Most of us fall somewhere within two different approaches. There are those within the church who regard the Bible as a divine product, authored word-by-word by God to be revered as literal, factual truth. Others see the Bible as divinely inspired responses of Israel and the early church to their encounters and understanding of God communicated through historical narrative, myth, and metaphor.

    This search for a biblical response to homosexual persons puts us face-to-face with the prior question: How do we understand the Bible?

2. How will the seven passages that directly relate to homosexual behavior be interpreted? Genesis 19; Leviticus 18:22, 20:13; Deuteronomy 23:17-18; Romans 1:26-27: I Corinthians 6:9; and I Timothy 1:8-10.

3. Particular biblical themes were found relevant to discernment. They are the story of creation, including being created in the image of God; the meaning of grace; the centrality of covenant relationships; the importance of procreation; hospitality to the stranger; liberation of those who are oppressed; and the miracles of healing and conversion.

4. What would Jesus say or do? Christians share the conviction that Jesus is our clearest revelation of God's will, "the Word made flesh." Yet, we have no direct teaching from Jesus about homosexuality. Given what we know about Jesus, what do we think his stance would be on this matter? What does being "in Christ" mean with regard to the church's response to gays and their families?

5. The study of non-biblical resources on homosexuality. Other sources of information and interpretation can be studied. What is the understanding of homosexuality from the behavioral sciences? What has been the stance of the church toward homosexual persons through its history? What materials and resolutions are available from our denomination and from other denominations?

C. Additional pastoral care

Let your plan include increased attention to the care of the members, both from lay and clergy leaders. This conversation about homosexuality will be stressful. The more stress emerges, the more caring is required. For instance, leaders can be especially alert to members who are not feeling understood and valued. Listening to their questions, convictions, and feelings helps them to stay engaged in the discernment.

Include some minimal basic training of lay caregivers for this purpose. In this training, hone listening skills; reinforce the importance of open questions, not answers; foster sensitivity to the stages of this process; and use role playing to build confidence in caregivers not accustomed to stressful conversations. This broader base of caring leaders will lower anxiety throughout the congregation by joining with you to create a climate conducive to reasonable discourse.

D. Leaders of the process

We have thought together about leadership in section #3 of this chapter. Allow what you decide about leadership to be a part of the plan presented to the congregation. The multiple roles of leadership should be clear, not only to yourselves, but to the congregation as well.

E. Congregational Affirmation of the Process

Two affirmations from the congregation are important. One, gain agreement about the plan from the congregation or at least from a broad segment of the leadership. This will significantly reduce the anxiety. People will have a chance to respond to the plan before the plan is implemented. The plan, of course, can be revised along the way, but knowing what to expect is a gift you give the church--and to yourselves.

Second, include in your proposal the way any decisions will be made. Members need to know how they can influence outcomes. Agreement on the process of decision-making before implementation builds confidence.

Securing these agreements on process will take time. Expect resistance from members who are eager to engage the conversation. I venture that obtaining affirmation of the plan and the way decisions are made will save time and frustration in the long run.

This planning reflects my earlier appeal for a bifocal vision: focus on content, focus on process. The *way* you conduct this conversation together is as important as *what* you decide. One accents the truth of the gospel for our time; the other accents the way that truth is discerned.

F. Evaluation of the process

Build into your plan the way you will reflect on your process. The evaluation of your plan and its implementation provides an important occasion of learning. There will be regrets, insights, celebrations, and questions. The eagerness to get on with other tasks can sabotage the benefits from reflection. I encourage you to seize the opportunity by asking, "Well, how did we do?"

Questions to consider in evaluating the process are:

- How will the evaluation be designed?
- Who will lead the evaluation?
- How can members who invested in the conversation be participants in its evaluation?
- How can this period of reflection be framed in a way that invites constructive criticisms and affirmations?
- When is the best time for the evaluation and how long should we allot?

As you reflect on your congregation, you will think of other components to add to your plan. Allow these suggestions, gleaned from the experience of other congregations, to stimulate your own thinking about an effective process.

CHAPTER 16

Implementing the Plan

L ET'S IMAGINE YOU ARE NOW AT THE PLACE of implementation. You have
decided that you are ready to lead the congregation in a conversation
about your relationship with lesbian and gay persons. You have defined the
questions to be addressed and clarified the roles of leaders for the process.
And the plan for discussion has been both formed and accepted by a broad
base of leaders, if not the congregation.

In this section I am anticipating with you some of the likely challenges
you will face in implementing your plan.

1. VALUE THE CONTEXT OF WORSHIP

Sunday after Sunday in corporate worship you are reminded as a congregation of the covenants around which you gather: God's covenant to be
with us and for us; and in response, our covenant to be God's people in our
day; and your covenant as a church to be with and for each other. These
unifying commitments both transcend and honor the differences on issues
or decisions. You regularly gather, not just as members of an organization,
but as members of the body of Christ seeking to embody the mind and
spirit of Christ in the world.

Include in your corporate worship specific references to the discussion
being experienced about homosexuality. This places the dialogue under the
umbrella of your shared mission. Along with prayers for guidance, consider offering in prayer the anxieties, questions, pains, regrets, and hopes in this
conversation. Together as a worshiping community the primary question is
raised: What is the shape of our faithfulness to God with regard to gay men
and lesbians in our church and community?

Pastors will need to decide the role of preaching in this process of discernment. If preaching is a primary way pastors declare their point of view,
it runs the risk of diminishing the dialogical nature of this dialogue.

However, some ministers preach in a way that invites, not discourages, ongoing conversation. The sermon is one, but not the only way a pastor can make available their sense of God's leadership.

Like corporate worship, private prayer is also a resource. There is prayer as petition: "Lord, what would you have us do?"; as intercession: "God, guide our congregation during these days"; as confession: "God, forgive my impatience, my failure to understand the other." When respectful listening is difficult and the way forward unclear we often are driven to prayer and drawn to worship.

2. Work with the resistance

Resistance to change is inevitable. You know this from living. We feel our resistance when significant challenges to change are presented to us. Even hopeful changes require of us the letting go of established patterns. You can expect opposition to this planned process with its implications of change.

Resistance to this conversation may be in the form of questions, such as: "Why bring up a subject best left alone?" "Why now, not later?" You may hear it in statements: "I'm feeling pressured to discuss a topic that is uncomfortable for me." "This is a political issue and doesn't belong in the church." "Even discussing this will legitimize homosexual behavior." "We'll lose members over this." "I don't have time for this."

Working with the resistance is a crucial aspect of your leadership. This challenge is true with any proposed change. But talking about sexuality, in particular homosexuality, is very personal and private. The resistance will likely be pronounced.

As you deal with resistance, I remind you of three conventional truisms:

A. Be patient. You are ahead of the congregation. The plan that you have been discussing over a period of time will be presented to a largely unprepared congregation. Explanations will require retelling. Clarifications and interpretations must be repeated over and over because members will be at different levels of understanding, both about the process and about the content of the discussion. Your capacity to maintain a calm, unhurried pace will be tested.

B. Honor the resistance. Respect it. Embrace it. Even go with the resistance. Know that somewhere within resistance there is an important value being protected. Ralph Waldo Emerson, in a playful statement, made the point well: "When a dog is chasing after you, whistle for him."

This stance is counterintuitive for most of us. By instinct we either avoid the resistance or attempt to overpower the resistance. Both, we know from life experience, are counterproductive. To avoid or to overpower will only strengthen the resistance. If no one responds to our concerns, then we are likely to amplify the volume of protest. If someone tries to out maneuver us or overtake us with superior force, then we dig in our heels all the more. Willful power invites willful resistance.

Working with resistance requires respect for the resister. It means you are willing to listen to the resisting voice until you comprehend the truth being valued. Resisting persons are protecting something important to them that they fear losing. The goal is to be understanding. You are saying to these members: "I care for you enough to understand what you are feeling or thinking. Furthermore, I am willing to be influenced by the concerns you are expressing, and I will work at listening until you feel taken seriously." Understanding does not mean agreement. It does mean being heard and valued completely. Agreement is not a prerequisite for staying in dialogue. Respect is.

C. *Stay focused* on the goals of the conversation. Some members may not budge from their resistance regardless of the respectful listening offered to them. They may refuse to be open to the dialogue. Then, the leaders' challenge becomes staying focused on the question. Giving undue power to intransigent resistance runs the risk of sidetracking the intent and movement of the process.

If dialogue about homosexuality breaks down with some members, I encourage you to seek other ways to remain in relationship. Church ministry provides multiple opportunities to stay connected. This is one advantage of having this dialogue in a congregational context. Along with this conversation about your relationship with gays and lesbians, the church is busy responding to personal and family crises, providing ongoing educational programs, reaching out in service to the larger community, managing its complexity through numerous committees, and grounding it all with regular services of worship. Apart from the discussion about homosexuality, there are numerous ways to maintain contact with members. Look for them.

3. Offer a non-anxious presence.

There will be anxiety if you choose to proceed. However, your presence within the congregation can be non-anxious. In the public arena the quality of your presence will either elevate or lower the anxiety among members. You function like a thermostat. If your anxiety is high, then the congregation becomes more anxious with you. If your anxiety thermostat is low, this also lowers the anxiousness in others, allowing for more reasoned exchanges of opinions and feelings. Clear thinking and emphatic listening are impossible in a highly anxious climate. The secure, calming presence of the leaders is often underestimated. You can remember a leader, perhaps a parent, a pastor, or a president, who in a time of crisis was able to lower your fears by conveying a confident stance. This centered, hopeful presence in the midst of emotional intensity is a critical gift you can bring to the conversation.

4. Work at self-definition.

The concept of self-definition is lifted from a view of leadership from family-systems theory articulated by Murray Bowen and interpreted for religious systems by Edwin Friedman. (The importance of a non-anxious presence also comes from this theoretical point of view.) From this perspective, leaders are challenged to focus on clarifying what they think, value, and believe in contrast to focusing on what others ought to think, value, and believe.

This also is counterintuitive. As leaders we tend to focus on leading the congregation to a particular goal. We define what the church ought to become. We concentrate on a specific outcome and attempt ways to get others to that point.

I am suggesting an alternate way of embodying leadership. I am encouraging you to focus on your own learning and understanding and offer it from this stance: "This is what I believe to be true; what do you believe to be true?" The leader speaks from an "I" position, not a "you" position, along with the faith that the ensuing dialogue, while full of differences, will lead toward mature choices. You give up the illusion of control by trusting that many eyes for seeing are better than one eye. The Spirit, I trust, is active in this mutual search for God's will. The outcome, currently unknown, will be the product of a process in which members commit to self-definition and listening, that is, "This is what I see . . . what do you see?"

I have witnessed two styles of communication from leaders that are *ineffective*. One, the church leader refrains from letting members know her or his questions and convictions about the inclusion of lesbians and gay men. They may fear unduly influencing the outcome of the discussion. But I think the church deserves to know where you stand as leaders. Of course, where you stand at one point may change as the dialogue continues. Honestly sharing your point of view stimulates, not stifles the conversation. This is true only if you declare your view with an open, inviting hand and not with a clenched fist of certainty. Your self-definition challenges others to do the same. By taking responsibility for your convictions, you invite members to take responsibility for their convictions. Whatever the particular outcome, the congregation grows in its capacity to discern their collective wisdom through a respectful, honest dialogue.

A second ineffective stance for the leader is to define others with the tone, "This is what you should believe. This is what God wants us to do. Don't you see it?" This invites either unthinking obedience or spirited resistance. Either way, those defined will abdicate responsibility for their own thinking.

I am offering an understanding of leadership that summons members to a high level of maturity. They will use your best thinking as leaders to clarify their own thinking. You will use their best thinking to clarify your own. Then together you discern your best sense of faithfulness in what emerges through the ongoing dialogue.

You can expect that some members will prefer to react to others rather than do the hard work of defining themselves. Mistakenly, they may experience your "this is what I see" as a coercive pressure for agreement. In some instances this will happen, but most people will respond to your respect for their capacity to sort out their own convictions.

I have defined my understanding of leadership. What is your response? What makes sense? What doesn't? How do you define effective leadership?

5. THINK THEOLOGICALLY.

The conversation about homosexuality and homosexual persons invites theological thinking. You may feel this challenge a bit foreboding until you realize that you are already theologians serving a church full of theologians. All of us carry explicit and implicit assumptions about the will of God, the person of Jesus, the interpretation of scriptures, the understanding of human nature, the work of the Spirit, and the mission of the church. This open dialogue about the church's relationship with same-gender persons will lift to the surface some of these assumptions, allowing members to sort through, revise, and reaffirm them.

As leaders, you can help the congregation to think theologically. You are not leading a political or sociological discussion. You are directing a process of discerning God's Spirit among you. This conversation can be an exercise in theological reflection if you keep an eye on the possibility. As you lead this process, consider looking for opportunities to frame this conversation theologically.

I'll offer some examples. Within your process of discernment, prayers will request that God's will be done. You can look for occasions to ask, "There are images about the nature of God in our praying. What are they?" "Where do we look for God's will?" "Have there been times when you felt confident about God's will? How do those experiences relate to our conversations about relationships with gays and their families?"

Members will be talking about what the church should do. It deepens the discussion to ask, "What do we see the purpose of the church to be? What's our mission in our time, in our community? How does this dialogue about homosexuality fit with our understanding of Christ's mandate to us as his disciples?"

There is no evidence that Jesus spoke about our response to homosexual persons. Neither did he address directly the issues of women in ministry or abortion or our relationships with Muslims. Yet, as the church in our day, we are making decisions about these concerns. We are asking, "What would Jesus do if he were physically present with us?" "How did his way of relating to others shed light on our relationships with persons of same-gender orientation?"

Questions about human nature are inevitably raised. Are homosexual persons created in the image of God? If so, what difference does that make in our attitudes? Is sexual orientation a choice or is it a discovery? Can Christ change one's sexual orientation from homosexual to heterosexual? Is homosexual behavior always a sin? When does sexual behavior fall short of God's intention for us?

The opportunities for theological reflection will abound in this dialogical search for moral guidance. As leaders, you can be sensitive to these openings for clarification and deepening of faith.

6. Support leadership.

Your leadership and the leadership of others are key to an effective, respectful conversation. You will set the climate, clarify the goals, interpret the plan, frame the questions, and offer a steady, confident presence in the midst of the discussion. Therefore, the support you need must be factored into your planning.

As you proceed, I hope that you keep your eye on each other and others who assume leadership positions. Look for signs of fatigue and needs for encouragement. Sharing both the anxiety and responsibilities of leadership will make possible the patient care required in this conversation.

The leadership team provides a place for prayer, planning, and reviewing the implementation of the plan. It also can be a community of mutual support. Checking on each other's welfare is as important as the periodic assessment of the process.

Once again, I ask you to add to my speculations. As you imagine yourselves implementing your planned process, what other needs come to your mind? How would you name the challenges before you?

This completes the section on leading the process of discernment. Only you and your congregation will determine *what* you decide to do. But the *when* and *how* of this process can draw from the wisdom of other congregations who have walked a similar path. Their wisdom I have attempted to articulate and offer.

SECTION III

Study Guide

THIS DISCUSSION GUIDE IS FOR those wanting to study whether your church should have this conversation about your relationship with homosexual persons and, if so, how you would proceed with a plan and its implementation. Both Sections I (The Pullen story) and Section II (Leading the Process) will serve as reference sources for the discussions. The themes for the study sessions parallel the chapters in Section II: Readiness, anticipating the stages, leadership, creating a plan, and implementing the plan.

The study guide is designed for an eight-week study. I picture a group of six to eight participants who will meet once a week for two hours. An alternative format could be a weekend retreat. I suggest specific reading assignments from Section I and II as preparation for each session. The study sessions will require a convener who plans for each meeting and facilitates the discussion. Note that each session includes more questions for study than can be addressed in the time allotted. The convener will select the questions that are most relevant to your situation.

Gathering and Clarifying Your Purpose

1. The goal of the first session is to clarify expectations and begin building a learning community. The convener can draw upon these suggestions in planning.

2. Ask participants to share their names, a brief statement about their history with the congregation, and their reasons for committing to this study.

3. Discuss the covenant you are forming. What agreements will encourage full participation? Consider the following: regular prayer for the work of the group; a pledge of confidentiality; commitment to attendance and preparation for each session; norms for communication, such as speaking for self, listening for understanding, and respect for differences; determining the place of prayer and worship within each study session.

4. Review and clarify the goals for the study. Ask the participants to reflect privately on the hopes and concerns they bring to this experience. Then record on newsprint in separate columns both the hopes and concerns of the group. Review together the patterns of similarity. Note also the differences. From the discussion, strive for clarity of goals to which everyone can commit.

5. Save the last fifteen minutes of the group time to discuss the questions, "How did we work together tonight? As we look to future meetings, what would you want more of, less of?"

6. Review preparation for Session #2.

Readiness

The goal of this session is to examine your sense of the congregation's readiness for an open conversation about your response to homosexual persons and their families. Is it time to proceed?

Preparation for Study Session #2: Read "Readiness" (chapter 1 in Section II) plus the references in the Pullen story selected by the convener for discussion. The convener can choose from the following questions in designing this second meeting.

A. QUESTIONS TO CONSIDER

1. In the Pullen narrative there were three particular times when the leaders struggled with the question of readiness: the decision of the deacons to support a churchwide forum on homosexuality (pp. 53–54); my decision to take Ron and Eric's request to the deacons (pp. 65–71); and the deacons' decision to take the request to the congregation (pp. 72–76). Where do you see similarities with your situation? Where do you see differences?

2. In the section "Readiness" (pp. 147–50), I lift up three questions: Is an open consideration of your relationship with gay members congruent with the mission of your church? Are your relationships between pastor and congregation, between leaders and congregation, and among members strong enough to value differences in the mutual search for God's will? Are there residual, unsolved issues that might be laid on top of this conversation in a distracting or destructive manner? Discuss these questions. Can you think of other issues that impact your readiness for this larger discussion?

B. Counting the Cost and Blessings

3. Both cost and blessing were consistent threads running throughout the Pullen narrative. This theme is specifically addressed in the epilogue (pp. 142–44). How do you think Pullen's consequences will compare with your experience if you choose to proceed?

Discuss the potential benefits from this open conversation. In *Readiness* (pp. 149–50), I identify these possible blessings: membership renewal, theological education, deepening of worship life, evangelistic opportunities, and strengthening the congregation's capacity for dialogue and decision-making. Do you see these as realistic possibilities? What is not included that you predict in your experience?

Review preparation for Session #3 and reflect on the way you related and worked together in this session.

Anticipating the Stages

The goal of this session is to help you reflect on the stages that you can expect to experience, both within yourselves and within the congregation. Each anticipated stage is a focus for study and comment.

Preparation for Study Session #3: Read "Anticipating the Stages" (chapter 2 in Section II) plus the references in the Pullen story selected by the convener for discussion. The convener may choose from the following questions in designing this third meeting.

1. In the Pullen story (pp. 28–29, 62–63) you experienced both Darrell, the business man, and Gary, the minister, who came to me asking for only one visit. They wanted another human being to know the truth about their sexual orientation. To share with others their long-kept secret seemed a cost too high for them. Discuss their decisions to remain "in the closet." Can you put yourself in their place and talk about what you might feel and do?

2. In my journal entries (pp. 59–60) I wrote about Lee's amazement that he could be loved by God. It was the beginning of going public and eventual baptism. And I described the parents, Jim and Francis, who had been stunned by their daughter's announcement that she is lesbian (pp. 25–26). Do these stories resonate with your experience of the coming-out process?

3. Consider inviting an openly gay person or parents of gays, preferably members from the congregation, to tell their coming out experiences. What stages do you detect in their stories?

4. In the Pullen story (pp. 21, 23, 24) I interpret my first sermon on homosexuality and my first "Point of View" article in the local newspaper as my coming out of the closet. In what way is your current

study of homosexuality a "coming out of the closet" experience for you? What early stages of this transition do you see?

5. In the Pullen narrative (pp. 53–54) Pat Long shared with the leaders of Pullen (deacons) her story as a closeted lesbian who had come to understand and accept God's love for her as she is. She also requested that the topic of homosexuality be open for study by the congregation. What are the advantages and disadvantages of her way of breaking the silence within a church? Can you detect the stages of the coming-out process in the actions that followed her openness? Imagine with each other the various ways that this topic of homosexuality might be introduced within your congregation.

6. In the deacons' letter to the Pullen congregation that introduced Eric and Ron's request, along with a recommended process, the leaders, in effect, "outed" the congregation as a faith community openly discussing their relationship with gays (pp. 80–93). Where in this story do you note the stages of confusion, listening for understanding, thinking for conviction, and realignment of relationships? Which stages in the Pullen narrative seemed to be handled more or less effectively than others? What connections are you making from the stages in Pullen process with your own imagined experience with your congregation?

7. My written narrative of the Pullen story ends before the final stage of integration and, in some instances, reconciliation. There is evidence of this stage in the acceptance of differences within relationships, particularly in the experience of Mike Watts (p. 140). He opposed the action of the congregation yet affirmed the worth of the process. Do you anticipate in your church persons like Mike Watts who can disagree with decisions yet maintain strong relationships in common commitment to the church's ministry? Can you think of instances in your own congregation when such maturity was displayed?

8. Having reviewed in "Anticipating the Changes" (pp. 151–54) the stages of confusion, listening for understanding, thinking for conviction, realignment in relationships, and integration, which do you see as the greatest challenge for your congregation? In what way does anticipating these stages make a difference in your desire to proceed with this process of discernment?

Review preparation for Session #4 and reflect on the way you related and worked together in this session.

Leadership

The goal of this session is to assess the leadership of your process. If you proceed with an open conversation, what kind of leadership will be required?

Preparation for Session #4: Read "Leadership" (chapter 3 in Section II) plus the references in the Pullen story selected by the convener for group discussion. The convener will choose from the following questions in designing this fourth session.

1. In both the Introduction (p. 12) and in the chapter on Leadership (pp. 155–58), I express the conviction that "how this conversation is conducted is as important as *what* is decided." I appealed for leadership from this bifocal perspective. Discuss your response to my conviction. In what ways would the process be as important as the content of information shared or decisions made?

2. I suggest in this section the value of a representative leadership team that is assigned the responsibility of overseeing this process (pp. 155–56). Would a leadership team make sense in your situation? If so, what leadership functions need to be represented? Do people in your congregation come to mind that might fill these roles?

3. In the Pullen story I explain my self-understanding as pastoral leader (pp. 71–73, 94). As you speculate about an open conversation, how would you define the pastor's role? As clergy, how do you see your leadership? As laity, how do you see the pastor's role?

4. In Pullen's process the leadership of Pat Long was significant (pp. 53–55, 74). There was also influence from other gays like Joy (p. 87) and Bill Brantley (pp. 50–52, 55–56). How do you assess the impact of their leadership? Are there gay men and lesbians in your congregation

who acknowledge openly their sexual orientation? Are they respected members of the congregation? What role, if any, would you anticipate them having in the discussion?

On page 157 I introduced the phrase "leading from the past." This concept was my awareness recorded as a journal entry (pp. 74, 75). We discovered actions in Pullen's tradition that supported the risk of defining the church's relationship and homosexual persons.

Are there times in your congregation's heritage when some controversial concern was addressed? What happened? How were differences handled and decisions made? How might these experiences from your past inform your current consideration?

In Pullen's experience the media played a prominent role. Discuss the way Pullen worked with the media (pp. 77, 80, 81). How could we have been more effective in working with them?

If you proceed with your open conversation, do you anticipate interest from the media, either secular or denominational? What can you draw from Pullen's experience with the media that fits your situation?

Review the list of possible uses of consultation in the chapter on Leadership (p. 158). Which ones might you draw upon? Can you think of other outside assistance not included on the list?

Review the preparation for Session #5 and reflect on the way you have worked together in this discussion.

Creating a Plan

Part 1

The goal of this session is to assist you in thinking about a plan. What components need to be included in the way your congregation would conduct this conversation?

Preparation for Session #5: Read "Creating a Plan" (chapter 4 in Section II) plus the references in the Pullen story selected by the convener for group discussion. The convener may choose from the following questions in designing this fifth session.

1. In Pullen's case there were two plans. One was a request made to the deacons to begin an educational process within the congregation (pp. 53–58). A second request came to me as pastor. I forwarded this request for the blessing of a same-gender union to the deacons with my support, and after considerable discussion, they presented their recommendations to the congregation (pp. 73–76). In these instances, how clear was the question being discussed? Did the deacons and later the congregation understand the purpose of the dialogue and decisions to be made? What can you learn from Pullen's experience?

2. You may be considering a response to a request, or a question regarding the church and homosexuality may be rising from among yourselves as leaders. After reviewing the list of questions in "Creating a Plan" (pp. 159–60) do any of these approximate the questions you are considering? How would you phrase your primary question(s)?

3. In the Pullen narrative there were decisions made about a time line. Decisions about the time line continued to be debated, particularly regarding the request from Eric and Ron (pp. 75, 90, 107). Discuss your response to the issue of timing in Pullen's experience. Did the leaders attempt a process that required more time than they allotted for it? Less time?

Think of a critical decision in your church's history. In the planning of that discussion was there an agreed-upon length of time? What did you learn from that experience that might inform your planning of this possibility?

5. The narrative of my journal entries is largely a string of life stories. There is an assumption that threads my presentation of the Pullen experience: regardless of one's conviction about the church and homosexuality, everyone has a composite of experiences, impressions, and questions about this subject. Everyone has a story to be received with understanding. Take note particularly of the fishbowl exercise and my commentary on its power (p. 30). Discuss your responses.

6. You may want to invite one to three guests to share their stories. These persons might be open gays within your congregation, family members of gays, persons willing to relate their ambivalent struggle for clarity, or leaders of other congregations who have engaged in this discussion.

7. Consider setting up the fishbowl exercise. Twenty to thirty members would be needed for this experience. Seek diversity in the gathering. Place six to eight chairs in a circle. Invite persons from the larger group to volunteer, sit in the circle and tell their personal perceptions, experiences, questions, opinions, or assumptions about homosexuality. Everyone is encouraged to speak from an "I," not "you" position. No debate, not even questions are allowed. Each story is received as a gift. After persons speak, they return to the larger group, freeing a place for another to join the circle. It's important that no one feel coerced to share. To structure such an experience may give you a sense of the congregation's readiness to proceed with this dialogue.

8. With this being the fifth meeting of your study group, there may be sufficient trust for you to share with each other your own history of attitudes, feelings, and thoughts regarding homosexuality. Again, the ground rule of "no debate" must be in place for this experience. The purpose is valuing and understanding each person's story. Once completed, you may want to discuss the impact of this self-revealing. What did it contribute to your study group?

9. After experiencing one or more of these suggestions, how do you envision the telling of personal stories in your planning? What structures would enhance the safety required for these experiences?

Review the preparation for Session #6 and reflect on the way the group worked together in this session.

Creating a Plan

Part 2

The goal of this session is to continue your thinking about a plan.

Preparation for Session #6: Complete reading "Creating a Plan" (Section II, chapter 4), plus the references in the Pullen story selected by the convener for this session. The convener will choose from the following questions in designing this sixth session.

1. Early in my pastoral responses I faced the role of scripture. "What does the Bible say?" was usually the first question raised by an inquiring Christian. Soon the question of how we interpret scripture (hermeneutics) came to the forefront (pp. 19, 20, 31, 32, 60, 61). In what way does my personal struggle with the biblical perspective on homosexuality parallel your own? Where do you experience differences?

2. In the Pullen experience a forum on homosexuality was established that included the response of the church in history, and the current scientific understanding of homosexuality, along with biblical and theological reflection (pp. 56–59) How would you evaluate the role the forum played in Pullen's process? Does it suggest ideas for an educational event in your congregation?

3. In "Creating A Plan" (p. 162) I suggest six areas of study: how we interpret the Bible; the specific biblical references to homosexuality; other biblical themes relevant to the conversation; the sense of Jesus' response; the view of homosexuality in church history; and the understanding of homosexuality from the behavioral sciences.

    As you envision a plan, how would you offer occasions for study? What questions do you anticipate that will call for informed attention?

Are there those within the congregation or beyond who can lead this study?

4. Observe in the Pullen story how the deacons introduced their plan to the congregation (pp. 75–77). Was the congregation clear about how and when decisions would be made regarding Eric and Ron's request? Are there points in the Pullen process that you could incorporate? How would your approach differ?

5. In "Creating A Plan" (p. 163), I recommend that your plan include the requests for two confirmations of the process: first, the approval of the plan by the congregation or at least a broad segment of the leadership; and second, the agreement on how any decisions about outcomes of this process will be made.

   What is the benefit of gaining wide affirmation of the planned process before proceeding with the discussion? What is the downside? In your congregational experience, who tends to decide how a process of discussion and/or decisions will occur? Does this historical pattern seem appropriate for this occasion?

6. In the Pullen experience, I express my surprise over the additional pastoral care required. In "Creating A Plan" (p. 163), I suggest minimal training of lay leaders in respectful listening. Would that be helpful in your situation? Where in your congregation do you anticipate the need for increased personal attention ?

My journal entries conveying the Pullen story end prior to an intentional evaluation that came later. In "Creating A Plan" (p. 164), I list questions to consider in evaluating the process. Discuss their relevance for your plan.

Review the preparation assignment for Session #7 and reflect on the way you worked together as a study group.

Implementing the Plan

For this session let's assume that a plan has been designed. The goal of this session is to anticipate the challenges you will likely face in implementing your plan.

Preparation for Study Session #7: Read "Implementing the Plan" (chapter 5 in Section II) plus the references in the Pullen narrative selected by the convener for discussion. The convener may choose from the following questions in designing this seventh session.

1. Review the place of corporate worship in the Pullen story (pp. 94–96, 100–102, 133, 134) Does Pullen's experience help you clarify the role of corporate worship within your process? What would be similar or different?

2. In "Implementing the Plan" (pp. 165–66), I describe corporate worship as the gathering where common covenants with God and each other are renewed. These unifying commitments, I suggest, both transcend and embrace the differences over particular issues, such as homosexuality. Can you think of instances when the affirmation of enduring commitments in worship has provided the cohesion during stressful times?

3. In times of serious discussions within your congregation what has been the role of prayer? How will you include encouragement and guidance to pray in your implementation?

4. In the Pullen narrative, working with resistance from both within and beyond the congregation was a central challenge to the leaders. This was particularly the case when the church was discerning their response to Eric and Ron's request. Pastoral responses and use of church newsletters are examples of addressing and honoring the resist-

ance (pp. 88, 89, 92, 93, 97, 98, 112, 113). Discuss their effectiveness and relevance to your situation.

5. Think of a time either in your work or congregational setting when you were resistant to a proposed significant change. What did you do? What helped or hindered the management of your resistance? Or, you may prefer to recall a time when you were the one proposing the change. How did you work with the resistance you encountered?

As a group you may want to list on newsprint the responses from the group, both the examples of resisting and the instances of working with the resistance of others. Then ask: How do our past experiences with resistance influence our current understanding of leadership?

6. On pages 166–67 I offer three guidelines: be patient, honor the resistance, and stay focussed on the goals of the plan. Discuss their usefulness to your leadership. What guidelines would you add?

7. At significant moments in our Pullen process, I describe the confident, non-anxious presence of deacon chairperson Jim Powell (pp. 72–77, 89, 103). What difference did his sense of presence make in the discernment process? How does such leadership impact the way you may choose to lead?

8. A leader's calming presence in public is a critical gift that influences the process (p. 168). Test this assertion by recalling a crisis within your family, church, or our nation. Remember the difference that a leader's calm, non-anxious presence made to the level of creative, thoughtful responses. Recall, as well, an instance when the leader exudes anxiety, distrust, or defensiveness. Talk among yourselves about the differences in these experiences and how they might relate to the implementation of your plan.

9. In "Implementing the Plan" I introduced a concept of leadership that may seem unfamiliar. This understanding of leadership assumes that when leaders define and offer their point of view, this in turn invites others to define more clearly their understanding. I wrote, "The outcome, currently unknown, will be the product of a process in which members commit to self-definition and listening, that is, "This is what I see . . . what do you see?' . . . [This] summons members to a high level of maturity . . . [by challenging them to take] responsibility for their own convictions" (pp. 168–69).

Note the influence of this theory of leadership in two sections of the Pullen narrative: first, my work of self-definition before I took the request from Eric and Ron to the deacons with my recommendation (pp. 69–73); and second, the deacon's work at their self-definition (pp. 73–76) before presenting their recommendations to the congregation. Discuss your assessment of this understanding of leadership. What's useful, and what's not useful, about this way of viewing leadership?

10. Is self-definition occurring within your study group? Are you becoming clearer, both individually and as a group, about your thinking concerning homosexuality and the church? If so, how has that come about? How will your experience of learning with each other affect the way you might lead your congregation?

11. In my journal recording of the Pullen story, I express my surprise over the rich theological fervent that our discernment process generated (pp. 97–98, 120). The discussion about homosexuality challenged the church to review its understanding of God, scripture, Jesus, the mission of the congregation, and the work of the Spirit.

As you implement your plan, what theological questions can you imagine being raised? Is this an educational dimension you want to anticipate and emphasize?

12. In writing the Pullen narrative, I singled out the personal support that I received as a leader (pp. 99, 100, 114–16). As you envision leading this process, what needs for support can you anticipate? What would be the nature of that support? How might support to leaders be built into the implementation of your plan?

Review the preparation for the final session, #8, and reflect on the way you have worked together as a study group.

Concluding the Study

The goal of this session is to summarize your learnings from the past eight weeks, project plans for the future, and bring closure to the group experience.

Preparation for Study Session #8: Come prepared to discuss the following questions:

1. From your eight-week study, do you believe that your church is ready to proceed with some form of open conversation about your relationship with homosexual persons and their families? Be willing to explain your answer.

2. What is clearer to you about how such a process of discernment might be lead in your congregation?

Review the movement of this study by recalling the topic and discussion of each session.

One purpose of the study was to assess the readiness of your congregation for considering its relationship with gays and their families. Ask the members of the group to share their responses to the first question: "Do you believe our church is ready to proceed with some form of open conversation?" List on newsprint a summary of each person's thinking. Listen for clarity, themes, further questions, and any consensus on the readiness to move forward with a plan.

Similarly, proceed with the second question: "What have we learned about how to lead a process of discernment?" The members of the group will offer their learning, summarized on newsprint. In the discussion after each person has shared, look for common threads, differences, further questions, and implications for leadership.

Having discussed the responses to both questions, is there agreement about next steps? If so, what are they?

Allow time for members of the study to reflect on their own process. How did we work together? What regrets? What appreciations? What affirmations?

Close the meeting with a time of worship, including scripture reading and prayer.

Annotated Bibliography

The following books and articles directly relate to congregations discerning their response to gay and lesbian persons.

Gaede, Beth Ann, ed. *Congregations Talking about Homosexuality.* Herndon, Va.: An Alban Institute Publication, 1998. This collection of essays is a practical resource for congregational leaders considering an open conversation in their congregations about homosexuality. The contributors combine guidelines along with case studies of seven congregations that have engaged this discussion.

Glennon, Fred. "Must a Covenantal Sexual Ethic Be Heterocentric? Insights from Congregations," in *Perspectives in Religious Studies* 28, no. 3 (Fall 2001): 215–33. The writer argues that the ethical norm of covenant includes both those of homosexual and heterosexual orientation. He draws supporting examples from the process of two congregations, Oakhurst Baptist Church in Atlanta, Georgia, and Pullen Memorial Baptist Church in Raleigh, North Carolina.

Hartman, Keith. *Congregations in Conflict: The Battle over Homosexuality.* New Brunswick, N. J.: Rutgers University Press, 1996. This book examines the internal struggle of nine congregations as they faced their responses to homosexual persons. He examines the conflicts played out in these churches and, in some cases, their denomination. The writer describes how these conflicts were handled, and, in some instances, resolved.

Oliveto, Karen P., Kelly D. Turney, and Traci C. West. *Talking About Homosexuality.* Holy Conversations: A Congregational Resource series. Cleveland, Ohio: The Pilgrim Press, 2005. This book provides a challenging and creative process for clergy and lay persons to reflect upon their own Christian beliefs and personal experiences through dialogue and study. Designed to be used in six two-hour sessions structured according to the Wesleyan quadrilateral—scripture, tradition, reason, and experience.

Polaski, LeDayne McLeese, and Millard Eiland. *Rightly Dividing the Word of Truth: The Congregational Response to Gay and Lesbian Persons.* Charlotte, N.C.: Baptist Peace Fellowship of North America, 2001. This resource includes the results of a retreat comprising representative leaders from thirteen Baptist congregations that had discussed their relationship to homosexual persons. The learning about how and when to have this discussion is included in the feature article. This book contains a wealth of sermons and articles as well as a bibliography organized by topics particularly pertinent to a congregational dialogue about homosexuality.

Siler, Mahan. "Blessings Unforeseen," in *Otherside* (Janurary 2002). This article is addressed to congregations that are at the point of possibly making explicit their implicit acceptance of gay Christians. By featuring the blessings from engaging this possibility, congregational leaders are encouraged to take the next step toward an open discussion.

Wink, Walter, ed. *Homosexuality and Christian Faith.* Minneapolis: Fortress Press, 1999. These short articles from church leaders address the moral imperatives about homosexuality. They include the specific challenges that churches face: the biblical witness and authority, the morality of sexual behavior, the dilemmas of families and friends of gays and lesbians, and the significance of covenants.